Making Refugee Self-Reliance Work

This book, along with any associated content or subsequent updates, can be accessed at https://hdl.handle.net/10986/43145.

Making Refugee Self-Reliance Work

From Aid to Employment in Sub-Saharan Africa

Johannes Hoogeveen
Karishma Silva
Robert Benjamin Hopper

WORLD BANK GROUP

ISBN (paper): 978-1-4648-1969-8
ISBN (electronic): 978-1-4648-2249-0
DOI: 10.1596/978-1-4648-1969-8

Cover: Given the opportunity to work, many refugees find gainful employment. Aime Dambou sells eggs from a kiosk in Bangui, Central African Republic.
Cover photo: © Stéphan Gladieu / World Bank. Further permission required for reuse.
Cover design: Bill Pragluski, Critical Stages, LLC

The Library of Congress Control Number has been requested.

Contents

Foreword   *xi*

Acknowledgments   *xiii*

Key Messages   *xv*

Executive Summary   *xix*

Abbreviations   *xxxv*

PART I: Setting the Context   1

Chapter 1: Generously Hosting Refugees in a Way That Creates Dependency 3

On the Need to Reform the Approach to Hosting Refugees   3

Refugees in SSA   7

Making Refugee Self-Reliance Work   14

About This Report   16

Notes   17

References   17

PART II: Self-Reliance as a Foundation for a More Efficient and Humane Approach to Hosting Refugees   19

Chapter 2: Using Poverty Lines to Measure Refugee Self-Reliance 21

Why Measure Self-Reliance?   21

Review of the Literature on Measuring Self-Reliance   22

Using Poverty Lines to Measure Monetary Self-Reliance   24

Refugees' Poverty and Self-Reliance in SSA   26

Conclusion   33

Annex 2A. Summary Statistics on Poverty and Self-Reliance among Hosts and Refugees   35

Notes   37

References   38

Chapter 3: Increased Refugee Self-Reliance and the Triple Win 39

Introduction   39

Estimating the Cost of Meeting Refugees' Subsistence Needs   40

Benchmark Cost of Subsistence Needs for Refugees in SSA   43
Refugees' Self-Earned Income   45
Humanitarian Assistance Needed and Provided   46
Filling the Shortfall in Humanitarian Assistance   48
A Triple Win   49
Conclusion   51
Notes   53
References   53

PART III: Making Refugee Self-Reliance Happen   55

Chapter 4: Country Vignettes on Self-Reliance. 57
Introduction   57
Uganda: Self-Reliance through Access to Land   57
Niger: Making Progressive Refugee Policies Work Even Better   65
Kenya: The Challenge of Ending Large-Scale Encampment   74
Chad: A Refugee Compact to Realize the Triple Win   86
Notes   94
References   96

**Chapter 5: Toward Greater Refugee Self-Reliance in
Sub-Saharan Africa 99**
Introduction   99
Aligning the Responsibilities of Host Countries and
    Humanitarian Agencies   100
Adapting Financing and Investment Models to Self-Reliance   101
Breaking the Curse of Encampment   104
Strengthening Refugees' Economic Inclusion   108
Investing in the Preparedness Agenda   112
Concluding Reflection: Leadership and Dialogue
    Are Key to Refugee Self-Reliance   113
Annex 5A. Policy Matrix for Greater Refugee Self-Reliance   116
Notes   119
References   119

**Appendix A: Background Papers and Data Sets
Prepared for this Report. 121**

Boxes
3.1   Measuring Refugees' Self-Earned Income   41
5.1   Refugee Camps over Time   107

Figures

ES.1   Self-Reliance among Hosts and Refugees   xxii

ES.2   Self-Reliance and Subsistence Aid Received by Poor Refugees
       as Share of the Poverty Line for Refugees Living in Different
       Locations   xxiv

ES.3   Percent of Refugees Living in Camps or Camp-Like Situations,
       Selected Regions   xxvi

ES.4   Key Elements to Promoting Refugee Self-Reliance   xxxi

1.1   Refugee Trends and Top-10 Refugee-Hosting Countries in SSA   4

1.2   Changes in Composition of ODA Provided by OECD
       Countries, 2018–21   5

1.3   Percent of Refugees Living in Camps or Camp-Like Situations,
       Selected Regions   7

1.4   Percent of Refugees in SSA Achieving Durable Solutions, 2014–23   8

1.5   Decomposition of Refugee Population, by Age and World Region   9

1.6   Location of Refugees, by World Region   10

1.7   Refugees' Work Rights in Law and in Practice, Selected
       Sub-Saharan African Countries   12

1.8   Refugees' Access to Education and Health Care, Selected
       Sub-Saharan African Countries   13

2.1   Poverty Incidence among Hosts and Refugees,
       Selected Countries   27

2.2   Aid Received by Poor Refugees per Year, Selected
       Countries and Locations   28

2.3   Cost of Reducing Refugees' Poverty by 1 Percentage Point,
       Selected Countries   29

2.4   Self-Reliance among Hosts and Refugees, Selected Countries   30

2.5   Refugee Self-Reliance, by Location, Selected Countries   31

2.6   Subsistence Aid Received by Poor Refugees as a Share of
       the Poverty Line, and Refugee Self-Reliance, Selected Countries   32

2.7   Self-Reliance and Subsistence Aid Received by Poor
       Refugees as Share of the Poverty Line for Refugees Living in
       Different Locations   33

3.1   Benchmark Cost for Refugees' Subsistence Needs and the
       Diminishing Need for Humanitarian Assistance with
       Increased Refugee Self-Reliance   42

3.2   Benchmark Amount of Humanitarian Assistance when
       Poor Refugees Are as Well-Off as Poor Hosts   43

3.3	Benchmark Cost of Subsistence Needs, by Country Income Category	44
3.4	Estimated Refugee Income, by Country Income Group	46
3.5	Annual Humanitarian Assistance to Make Refugees as Well-Off as Hosts, by Country Income Group	47
3.6	Sources of Consumption Financing Relative to the Poverty Line, Selected Countries	48
3.7	Distribution of ODA for Refugee Situations, Select SSA Host Countries, 2020–21	50
3.8	The Triple Win of Increased Refugee Self-Reliance	52
4.1	Self-Reliance, by Refugee/Host Status and by Refugee Characteristics, Uganda	59
4.2	Differences in Selected Characteristics across Host and Refugee Households, Uganda	62
4.3	Location of Origin for Refugees, Selected Countries in East Africa	65
4.4	Oaxaca-Blinder Decomposition of Log Income between Hosts and FDP Groups, Niger	71
4.5	Oaxaca-Blinder Decomposition of IDPs versus Nigerian Refugees and IDPs versus Malian Refugees, Niger	72
4.6	Self-Reliance for Refugees and Hosts, by Location, Kenya	78
4.7	Employment for Hosts and Refugees around Camps, Kenya	79
4.8	Comparing Welfare Outcomes for Refugees and Hosts Living Near Camps, Kenya	82
4.9	Refugees Present in Chad, 2002–25	87
4.10	Poverty and Self-Reliance, Refugees, Hosts, and Overall, Chad, 2018 and 2022	88
4.11	Self-Reliance, Subsistence Aid Received by Poor Refugees, and Humanitarian Funding, Chad, 2018 and 2022	89
4.12	Paid Humanitarian Resources, Chad, 2004–24	91
4.13	Disbursed Humanitarian Aid and Two Scenarios for the Cost of Hosting Refugees, Chad, 2004–24	92
5.1	Percent of Encamped Refugees in SSA, by Host Country Lending Category, 2024	102
5.2	ODA per Refugee, Largest ODA Recipients in SSA, 2020–21	103
B5.1.1	Number of Refugee Camps in SSA, by Size, 1999–2024	107
5.3	Key Elements to Promoting Refugee Self-Reliance	115

Tables

2.1	Microdata Sets Used	27
2A.1	Summary Statistics on Poverty and Self-Reliance among Hosts and Refugees, PPP$ 2.15	35
2A.2	Summary Statistics on Poverty and Self-Reliance among Hosts and Refugees, PPP$ 3.65	36
4.1	OLS Regression Results Explaining the Difference in the Log Ratio of Refugees' Nonhumanitarian Consumption to the IPL, by Refugee Household Characteristics, Uganda	60
4.2	Household Characteristics of IDPs, Refugees, and Hosts, Niger	67
4.3	Agricultural Inputs and Outputs for Refugee, IDP, and Host Households Engaged in Self-Employed Agriculture, Niger	69
4.4	Macroeconomic Effects on Turkana, Kenya, under Three Scenarios	77
5.1	Policy Dimensions Relevant for Refugees' Economic Inclusion	109
5A.1	Policy Matrix for Greater Refugee Self-Reliance	116

Foreword

A much-used proverb states, "Give a man a fish and you feed him for a day; teach him how to fish, and you feed him for a lifetime." For refugees, who often find themselves dependent on aid, living in remote camps with few economic opportunities, the adage remains as relevant as ever.

The refugee response needs a change in perspective. For far too long a care-and-maintenance approach has been the go-to way of dealing with refugee inflows, certainly in Sub-Saharan Africa. That approach has forced refugees into inactivity and dependence. Instead, it is more sustainable and cost-effective to build on their agency, skills, and readiness to take care of themselves. Such a development approach is particularly suited to protracted refugee situations until refugees can return in safety and dignity.

Formulating that change in perspective, this report argues that self-reliance should be at the core of the refugee response. Its message is extremely timely, coming at a moment when a humanitarian sector under financial duress explores new pathways for providing assistance to some of the most vulnerable people on the planet. The development approach proposed in this report not only is more durable and cost-effective but also presents a more humane, more dignified pathway for people whose only faults are having been at the wrong place at the wrong time and having to flee.

This report also makes a case for putting hosting governments in charge of the refugee response. Not only is it morally the right thing to do, but the option to hand over the management of refugees to humanitarian agencies to provide care and financing no longer exists. Instead of relying on parallel systems, a sustainable response model would emphasize inclusion in the economy and in national services along with the systematic channeling of financing for refugees through the treasury.

The report is groundbreaking in yet another way. By offering a definition for self-reliance that builds on the World Bank's tradition in poverty measurement, it lays the foundation for systematic monitoring and learning.

The global refugee response stands at an important crossroad; this report helps define a way forward and formulates a vision and an approach to which the World Bank is committed.

Andrew Dabalen
Chief Economist, Africa Region
World Bank

Acknowledgments

This report was produced by a core team consisting of Johannes Hoogeveen, Karishma Silva, and Robert Benjamin Hopper. It would not have come about without the support and contributions of many others. At the risk of omitting someone, we thank the various people who helped us analyze the data at hand as well as the coauthors on the background papers and data prepared for this report: Fikirte Abeje, Sebastian Anti, Aziz Atamanov, Cesar Cancho, Mohamed Coulibaly, Emilie Jourdan, Sebastian Leander, Olive Nsababera, Benjamin Reese, Jonathan Rigberg, Collette Salemi, Zara Sarzin, Aboudrahyme Savadogo, and Kristina Vaughan. Not only was it a great pleasure to work with each of you, we learned a lot from your insights and feedback.

A special thanks to Felix Schmieding of the Joint Data Center for very productive discussions on how to measure self-reliance and for promoting the idea that measures used to identify destitute nationals should also be relevant for forcibly displaced people; to Craig Loschmann, Maximilien von Berg, Gina Kosmidou-Bradley, and Betsy Lippman of UNHCR, the UN Refugee Agency, with whom we collaborated closely in various stages of this project; and to Irina Galimova (World Bank) for her consistent support and trust.

We would also like to mention Erwin Knippenberg, Tamar Appel, Annabelle Vinois, Farah Manji, Tom Bundervoet, and Xavier Devictor, for being available to exchange ideas and discuss various aspects of refugees' economic inclusion, as well as Fanette Blanc and Gabriel Mokate, for taking the time to explain UNHCR operations in Togo.

We extend our sincere gratitude to the entire editorial and production team including Amy Gautam, Talia Greenberg, Amy Lynn Grossman, Nora Mara, Jewel McFadden, and Anne Caroline Smith for their dedication and hard work in bringing this project to fruition.

Special appreciation to Johan Mistiaen, Rinku Murgai, Gabriela Inchauste, Luis-Felipe Lopez-Calva, and Andrew Dabalen for their guidance, support, and patience.

Finally, a special word of thanks to our sponsors, the World Bank–UNHCR Joint Data Center on Forced Displacement and the PROSPECTS Partnership Programme, funded through the World Bank–administered Multi-Donor Trust Fund for Forced Displacement, without whom this report would not have seen the light of day.

Key Messages

The Case for Promoting Refugee Self-Reliance

- **Refugee situations are development challenges.** Sub-Saharan Africa hosts 8.2 million refugees who, on average, have already spent 13 years in exile. These protracted situations require development-based solutions, not just humanitarian aid.

- **The care and maintenance approach to hosting refugees is costly and has perverse incentives.** Most funding supports refugees who, because of limited economic opportunities, are dependent on aid. This approach effectively rewards economic exclusion. A better approach rewards countries that promote refugee self-reliance and reduce aid dependence while shrinking the financial burden of hosting refugees.

- **Promoting refugee self-reliance represents one of the best opportunities to arrive at a sustainable refugee response model.** Self-reliance enhances refugee financial autonomy and reduces dependence on humanitarian assistance, allowing the available aid to be preserved for the most vulnerable. Financing for refugee situations is more productive when used to promote self-reliance and invested in development efforts benefiting hosts and refugees alike.

- **The best way to promote refugee self-reliance is through socioeconomic inclusion.** Nearly three-quarters of all refugees in Africa live in camps or camp-like settings, yet encamped refugees are the least self-reliant and most dependent on humanitarian assistance. By contrast, refugees who have the freedom to settle where they find economic opportunities perform much better.

- **Self-reliance requires inclusive policies.** Restrictions on refugees' movement or ability to work, or confining refugees to camps in remote areas, constrain their ability to earn and make their dependence on aid more substantial. Economic inclusion is more effective when coupled with freedom of movement and access to national services, which allow refugees to move to where economic opportunities best match their skills.

- **A shift to portable assistance improves refugee dispersion and reduces negative spillovers due to congestion.** Refugees tend to cluster in areas where assistance is provided. Refugees' ability to settle outside camps—that is, in places with the most favorable economic opportunities—is strengthened when assistance is portable instead of place based. Greater dispersion of refugees reduces the risk of negative spillovers on local economies and stress on local health and education services. Land-based strategies are also more likely to be effective when refugees can spread around.

- **The promotion of self-reliance by transforming camps into settlements and through area-based development strategies should be approached with caution.** Economic growth is typically unbalanced and concentrated in urban or peri-urban areas, and the potential for economic activity in remote locations is limited. Integrated settlements and area-based development are not likely to be very effective in promoting self-reliance; they may, however, be important to improving access to basic services for those living in isolated areas.

- **A shift to sustainable responses needs to be accompanied by a coherent, measurable understanding of what self-reliance entails.** This report defines refugees as self-reliant if their consumption from nonhumanitarian sources exceeds the poverty line,[1] implying that they generate sufficient income to pay for their consumption. This new measure is anchored in best practice for poverty measurement and uses the same welfare standard that applies to nationals.

- **Promoting self-reliance is the humane thing to do. It enhances the dignity of refugees and strengthens host governments and their economies.** Long recognized as the preferred way to host refugees, refugee self-reliance has remained elusive in practice. Increasing pressure on humanitarian funding can offer new impetus to boosting self-reliance and making refugee situations more sustainable.

A Policy Framework to Improve Refugee Self-Reliance

- **Government leadership is critical to realizing a new refugee hosting model. As with other development challenges, host governments must lead the refugee response.** Host governments can make sure they have in place an inclusive policy environment and can demarcate the roles and responsibilities of their development and humanitarian partners.

- **The shift to a country-led development approach to hosting refugees must be accompanied by development resources.** These resources should be predictable, rules-based, and channeled through government systems. Parallel and earmarked financing should be avoided. Host governments may require support for the recurrent costs they incur when including refugees in national systems, including those for health and education.

- **Host governments should take a strong policy stance against encampment.** Encampment leads to a wastage of human and financial resources. Money spent on handouts for refugees who are capable and ready to take care of themselves can be invested much more productively in growth and development, with benefits for hosts as well as refugees.

- **Host governments and the international community should invest in preparedness.** Many large refugee movements can be predicted. Emergency preparedness, including by dis-encamping refugees already on the territory, strengthens the efficiency and cost-effectiveness of hosting refugees in the initial phase of a crisis.

Executive Summary

Introduction

The refugee crisis in Africa is escalating, and pressures on host countries are mounting. As of 2024, Africa hosted 9 million refugees, a number that has soared in recent years, driven by conflicts and civil unrest. The civil war in Sudan resulted in the largest recent displacement crisis in the world, with over 10 million people forced to flee their homes and many seeking refuge in neighboring countries, including Chad, Ethiopia, South Sudan, and Uganda. Armed insurgencies in Burkina Faso, Mali, and Nigeria also contribute to the increasing number of refugees in the Sahel region. Conflict in the Democratic Republic of Congo in early 2025 has created further displacement in eastern Africa, with Burundi and Uganda seeing large new inflows. Most refugees originate from and resettle in poor localities, which can potentially tax host countries' limited resources. Nearly three-quarters (74 percent) of all refugees in Africa live in camps, often for protracted periods. More than 65 percent of refugees are poor, and few are self-reliant.

The existing refugee response system thus already struggles to deliver acceptable outcomes for refugees; worse, it is under increasing financial pressure. This pressure is the result of two concurrent developments. First, the global refugee population under the UN Refugee Agency's (UNHCR) mandate more than doubled, from 21.3 million refugees in 2021 to almost 32.0 million by mid-2024. Of these refugees, 28 percent live in Sub-Saharan Africa (SSA). Second, the amount of humanitarian financing available to address these challenges has been falling, reducing the amount available per refugee. Coupled with heavy reliance on a handful of donors, shifting policies among donor governments can severely disrupt humanitarian financing flows. Recent announcements point to a significant decline in external funding, and fiscal pressures among key donors suggest that this pattern will likely persist in the coming years.

Advocacy for refugee financing that keeps pace with the growing number of refugees remains crucial; however, the immediate challenge is to shift from a mindset focused on care and maintenance to one promoting development solutions to displacement. More specifically, there needs to be a move to sustainable interventions focused on economic inclusion and the promotion of self-reliance. This shift is reflected in the UNHCR's new vision, which goes under the moniker "Sustainable Responses." Sustainable Responses is about maximizing self-reliance and minimizing dependence on humanitarian aid by expanding the human potential of forcibly displaced people and supporting host governments to bring refugees into their national systems.

Sustainable Responses is anchored in host country leadership and premised on the promotion of refugee self-reliance. With refugees having already spent an average of 13 years in exile, refugee situations (beyond the emergency phase) not only are humanitarian crises but increasingly have become development challenges. As with other development challenges, host governments have to lead the refugee response to refugees. To do so, they should be supported in implementing policies and approaches that limit the financial and social costs of hosting refugees. This objective implies providing access to labor markets so that refugees can meet their subsistence needs through nonhumanitarian income. Economic inclusion is more effective when coupled with freedom of movement and access to national service provisions like health and education so that refugees can move to where jobs best match their skills. Any sustainable response model needs to simultaneously invest in countries of origin and in the safe and voluntary return of refugees to reduce the need for international protection over time. This shift to a country-led development approach must be accompanied by development resources directed to host governments.

A new refugee response model will need to deliver better outcomes with the available resources. That goal is feasible: if host governments provide refugees with better opportunities to earn incomes, refugees' dependence on aid to meet basic subsistence needs falls, saving critical humanitarian resources. This report estimates that if refugees earned 25 percent more than they do presently—which is realistic, given the gulf in earned income between refugees and hosts—the need for humanitarian assistance would decrease by $900 million annually in SSA alone. This amount is more than the annual outlay by the Window for Host Communities and Refugees, a funding mechanism of the International Development Association (IDA).

It is essential that the shift toward Sustainable Responses is accompanied by a coherent, measurable understanding of what self-reliance means. Without appropriate measurement, it is not only impossible to understand whether self-reliance has been achieved but also extremely difficult to build a body of evidence and generate the systemic learning required for it to be realized in the long run. Unfortunately, existing approaches to its measurement are at odds with the concept of self-reliance itself, because those approaches allow refugees who depend on humanitarian assistance to be considered self-reliant.

This report presents a new approach to measuring refugee self-reliance that defines refugees as self-reliant if their consumption from nonhumanitarian sources exceeds the poverty line. To be self-reliant, it is not sufficient for refugees to have a standard of living above the poverty line. Self-reliance requires that refugees generate the income necessary to attain a locally relevant, minimum standard of living without relying on humanitarian aid. It necessitates that refugees generate sufficient income to pay for their consumption, giving self-reliance a welfare connotation and reflecting the necessity to be active in the labor market. Because the proposed measure is anchored in best practice for poverty measurement and uses the same welfare standard used for nationals, it ensures comparability with host populations while signaling that for welfare purposes, refugees are not treated differently from their hosts.

African countries typically embrace self-reliance as a concept, even when in practice many refugees continue to face economic participation restrictions. The SSA region has been at the forefront of establishing a regional legal framework governing the protection and assistance of refugees and internally displaced persons with the 1969 Organisation of African Unity Convention and the 2009 Kampala Convention. Many SSA countries have domesticated provisions of these conventions into their national laws by closing camps, adopting new policies, including refugee children in public schools, and providing access to land and labor markets. Despite these efforts, substantial gaps remain between refugees' de jure rights and the de facto realization of those rights.

Refugees already meet a considerable share of their subsistence needs through earned income. This report shows that many refugees work. It estimates that refugees' earnings in SSA are equivalent to nearly 62 percent ($5.24 billion) of the $8.51 billion needed to bring the consumption of all refugees in SSA to the poverty line. Humanitarian aid given to refugees, by contrast, accounts for about 20 percent of these subsistence needs ($1.75 billion), implying a shortfall in assistance to refugees of $1.5 billion annually. This shortfall represents a lower-limit estimate because humanitarian spending goes not just to refugees; a nontrivial share goes to host communities.

Because of this shortfall and the lack of labor market opportunities, refugees in SSA have high poverty rates and low self-reliance rates in both absolute terms and relative to host populations. Poverty rates among refugees vary from 57 percent in Kenya to 75 percent in Ethiopia, compared to national poverty rates of 39 percent and 25 percent, respectively, in those countries. Self-reliance among refugees varies by country, from a high of 31 percent in Niger to a low of 14 percent in Uganda (figure ES.1). In comparison, self-reliance among nationals is found to be 54 percent and 63 percent in those countries, respectively.

Figure ES.1   Self-Reliance among Hosts and Refugees

Self-reliance among refugees is much lower than among hosts living nearby.

Self-reliance (%)

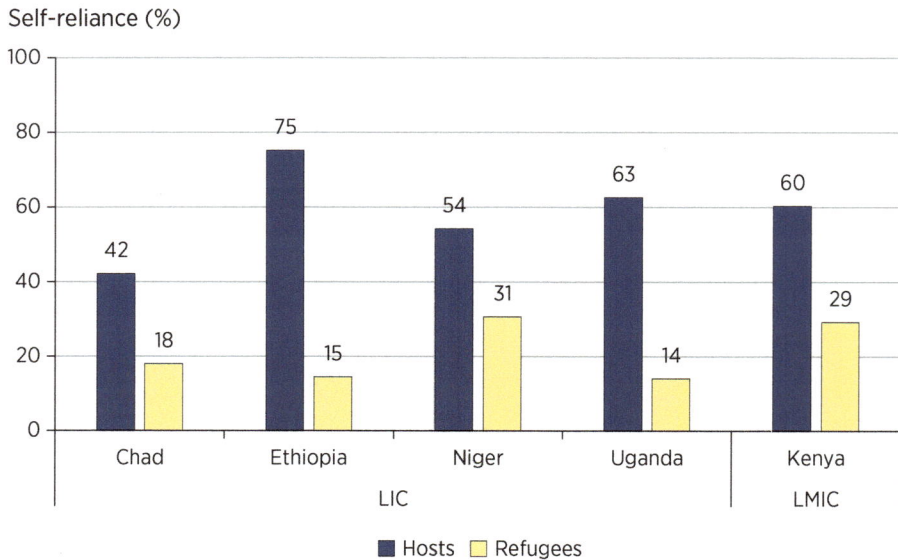

Source: Hoogeveen and Hopper 2024.

Note: The analysis uses the international poverty line of PPP$ 2.15 for low-income countries, including Chad, Ethiopia, Niger, and Uganda, and the global poverty line of PPP$ 3.65 for Kenya. LIC = low-income country; LMIC = lower-middle-income country; PPP = purchasing power parity.

Assisting Refugees: Aid versus Self-Reliance

Subsistence aid and self-reliance are complementary. When refugees face restrictions on movement—residing in camps or living in isolated areas with limited commercial activity—or are prohibited from working, their ability to participate economically is constrained, and the cost of meeting their subsistence needs through aid becomes more substantial than it would be otherwise. Conversely, when refugees are not confined to remote areas but settle, for instance, in urban areas where they have freedom of movement and are able to find work and profitable opportunities, their economic participation tends to increase. Similarly, this increase occurs when refugees are provided with the means to farm or herd livestock. In scenarios in which refugees meet (part of) their subsistence needs through earned income, their reliance on external assistance is reduced.

Refugees' poverty is more likely to be addressed through enhanced self-reliance than through increased aid. For refugees to meet their subsistence needs, aid would need to increase substantially: by 180 percent in Chad, 100 percent in Ethiopia and Uganda, approximately 120 percent in Kenya, and 250 percent in Niger. It is doubtful whether such increases in aid are realistic in the existing geopolitical context. By contrast, if the shortfall was made up by increased refugees' earnings, incomes would have to increase by 47 percent in Chad, 94 percent in Ethiopia, 34 percent in Kenya and Niger, and 64 percent in Uganda. Although still ambitious, these increases are achievable with the promotion of more sustainable approaches to refugees' inclusion.

Refugees demonstrate a preference for self-reliance. Self-reliance offers refugees a path to financial autonomy and the ability to build a future independent of aid. Many refugees who leave camps forgo substantial levels of aid. In Chad, poor refugees in N'Djamena receive 3 percent of the international poverty line in subsistence aid, versus the 15–19 percent received by refugees in camps (figure ES.2). In Ethiopia, the differences are even greater, with poor refugees in camps receiving on average 36 percent of the international poverty line, compared to 1 percent for those living in Addis Ababa. Poor refugees in Nairobi also receive, on average, 1 percent of the global poverty line, whereas those in Kalobeyei receive 33 percent. Although refugees in urban areas lower average poverty rates than those in camps, refugees leaving camps do not know ahead of time if they will be able to secure productive livelihood opportunities. By forgoing aid and risking poverty, they reveal a strong preference for self-reliance.

At least three distinct advantages are associated with increasing self-reliance among refugees. First, self-reliance reduces dependence on humanitarian assistance and improves the dignity and financial autonomy of refugees. Refugees who are self-reliant are more likely to return to their countries of origin once returning becomes feasible. Second, increased refugee earnings reduce the need for humanitarian aid, allowing it to be directed to the most vulnerable. Finally, savings from promoting refugee self-reliance can be reallocated to development efforts benefiting both hosts and refugees, fostering economic participation, growth, and social cohesion.

Promoting refugee self-reliance thus creates the scope for a triple win: (1) an increase in refugees' earnings and self-reliance, more aid for the most vulnerable refugees who are unable to work, and a decrease in poverty; (2) reduced aid dependence, which creates savings in the amount of humanitarian assistance required; and (3) scope to direct (part) of the savings on humanitarian assistance to accelerate development in host communities. This development aid can be used to address any potential negative impacts associated with greater inclusion of refugees, while stimulating economic activity and creating job opportunities for both host populations and refugees. Thus, scope exists for a mutually beneficial bargain between international donors and host countries.

Despite these apparent benefits, self-reliance among refugees in SSA remains low and efforts to support these activities remain elusive. To effectively address this challenge, it is important to delve into the factors that hinder self-reliance and engender high levels of dependence among refugees.

Figure ES.2   Self-Reliance and Subsistence Aid Received by Poor Refugees as Share of the Poverty Line for Refugees Living in Different Locations

Refugees living outside camps or camp-like settings are more likely to be self-reliant and receive less in aid than refugees who are encamped. The international community creates a perverse incentive by mostly spending on refugees who are constrained from realizing their economic potential, rather than on the dispersal of refugees and on investing in the development of host communities to the benefit of hosts and refugees alike.

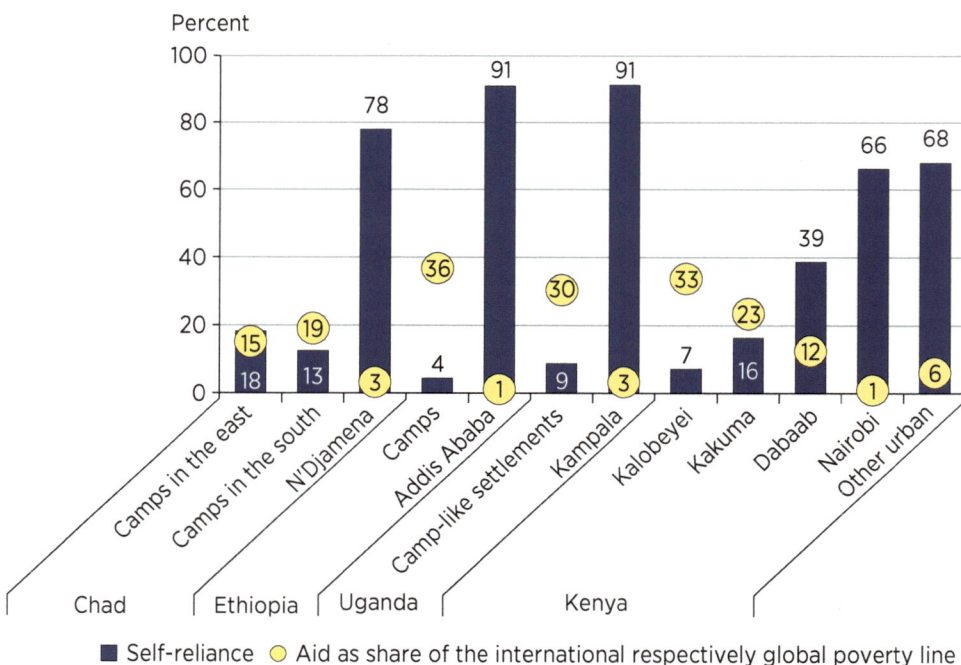

Source: Hoogeveen and Hopper 2024.

What Drives Low Self-Reliance among Refugees in SSA?

Barriers to refugee self-reliance are multifaceted and rooted in both policy and structural constraints. Forced displacement disrupts livelihoods, depletes assets, and diminishes human and social capital, leaving refugees in need of support to rebuild their productive capacity so they can meet their subsistence needs through self-earned income. Early policy decisions play a critical role in shaping refugees' outcomes. When host countries have inclusive policies, refugees are more likely to integrate into local economies and national service delivery systems. However, such policies often entail significant recurrent costs to the host government and may lead to negative spillovers. In resource-constrained settings—particularly in SSA, where public financing constraints are severe—governments may prefer to house refugees in camps, shifting the responsibility of their care to the international community. Consequently, even in countries with inclusive policies, camps or camp-like situations remain prevalent because they mitigate perceived security risks and place the burden of care on humanitarian partners, for whom camps make it easier to assess needs and deliver assistance.

Even without the creation of formal camps or settlements, refugees tend to cluster in informal settlements where humanitarian support is delivered. This tendency creates a cyclical problem: although many host countries in SSA have inclusive policy environments, they allow the establishment of camps or informal settlements because of inadequate financing. Once camps have been created and reach a certain size, they become hard to dismantle because (1) humanitarian agencies focus their assistance primarily through these camps; (2) host countries fear that their closure might create economic and social disruptions; and (3) refugees are reluctant to leave because doing so is risky, is costly, and leads to reduced access to aid. The combination of these factors leads to low levels of self-reliance and continued aid dependence even in countries with progressive refugee-hosting policies.

A large proportion of refugees in SSA is confined to camps (figure ES.3) and settlements situated in isolated and lagging areas with limited economic opportunities. Most camps are situated in remote areas, where refugees face food insecurity and limited access to livelihood opportunities, health care, and education; public service delivery is stretched; and it is more challenging to create employment opportunities. Poverty among encamped refugees is extremely high, ranging from 45 percent in Dadaab in Kenya to 84 percent among camps in Ethiopia, and poverty among hosts—typically those living within 15 kilometers of where refugees reside—is also very high. Although not as high as rates among refugees, poverty rates for host communities tend to exceed national poverty estimates: for instance, in Kenya, poverty rates (using national poverty lines) in Garissa and Turkana, where Kenya's refugee camps are housed, are 68 percent and 78 percent, respectively, compared to the national poverty rate of 39 percent (KNBS 2024). In Chad, poverty (using national poverty lines) among host communities is about 70 percent, compared to 42 percent nationally. Camps located in more remote areas characterized by fewer economic opportunities often demonstrate lower levels of self-reliance. In Kenya, self-reliance among refugees is lower in Kakuma (16 percent) and Kalobeyei (7 percent) than in Dadaab (39 percent), which benefits from closer proximity to population centers and trade routes. In contrast, refugees in urban areas tend to have higher rates of self-reliance than those in camp settings. For instance, in Ethiopia, self-reliance rates among refugees in camps are estimated at just 4 percent, compared to 91 percent among refugees in Addis Ababa. This situation highlights the limited economic opportunities that exist in and around camps or settlements for both refugee and host communities. It suggests that restoring the productive capacity of encamped refugees without improving the economic opportunities available to them is unlikely to lead to significant improvements in refugee self-reliance.

Figure ES.3   Percent of Refugees Living in Camps or Camp-Like Situations, Selected Regions

The percent of refugees living in camps or camp-like situations is highest in Sub-Saharan Africa. Unlike in Latin America and the Caribbean, which eliminated refugee encampment, the fraction of encamped refugees in Sub-Saharan Africa remained stable and increased more recently, driven by the conflict in Sudan.

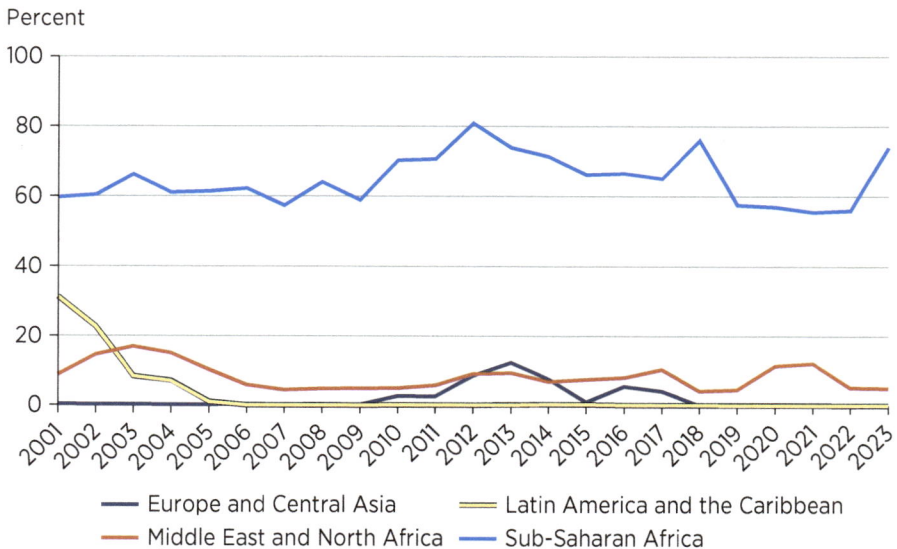

Source: Original calculations using data received from the United Nations High Commissioner for Refugees' Global Data Service.

Financing for refugee situations is not aligned with self-reliance objectives.
A large share (66 percent) of the official development assistance allocated to
refugee hosting is for humanitarian funding, even though only 22 percent of
refugees are in emergency situations, a mismatch that is particularly strong in
SSA. Moreover, large variations arise in the amount of aid refugees receive. Poor
refugees in Ethiopia, Kenya, and Uganda receive two to four times more aid, on
average, than those in Chad and Niger. Refugees residing in camps or
settlements tend to receive the most assistance, whereas refugees living outside
camps receive very little. In some situations, refugees in camps fare better than
those in their host communities. Finally, subsistence aid and self-reliance are
found to be inversely correlated. Settings in which refugees are less likely to be
self-reliant receive higher levels of aid; settings in which refugees are more self-
reliant receive lower levels of aid. Although this correlation makes sense from a
humanitarian perspective—that is, subsistence aid is given where it is most
needed—from a development perspective it suggests a perverse incentive in
that more aid is spent in environments where refugee self-reliance is hindered.
The challenge is to transform the current situation to one in which less
humanitarian assistance is needed because refugees are more self-reliant and
more development aid is used to incentivize self-reliance.

Lessons Learned from SSA

**Uganda's vision that refugees can contribute to the development of host
areas can be embraced more widely.** Uganda's approach promotes self-reliance
by providing refugees with plots of land in integrated settlements, offering a
sustainable source of livelihood that can reduce aid dependence. In addition, the
approach involves efforts to strengthen the local institutional capacity and
enhance service delivery in host areas to minimize disparities in access to basic
services and avoid tensions between refugee and host communities. The model
suggests that better economic and social integration of refugees and greater
access to productive assets such as land can increase self-reliance. In Chad,
refugees' economic integration in urban areas could be challenging given the
country's large number of refugees and its low level of urbanization. Chad's vast
territory and low population density make land-based inclusion approaches a
viable alternative. Chad could, in fact, borrow from Uganda's playbook and
consider refugees' economic inclusion a vehicle for rural development and
associated investments in connectivity and markets and improvements in
service provision.

For a land-based strategy to work, refugees need to be more dispersed.
Findings from Uganda reveal that only when refugees have access to sufficient
land do they become self-reliant. When refugees are concentrated in the same

location, access to fertile land inevitably becomes a constraint. Dispersion across the country means either more and smaller settlements or inclusion of refugees in existing villages. Many refugees originate from rural areas and are likely farmers or pastoralists. Provided with access to land or livestock, these refugees could be interested in spreading out across the country and integrating in rural communities that, in turn, may be interested in receiving refugees, especially when their arrival is associated with investments in local schools, clinics, and other public goods.

A shift to portable assistance can improve dispersion and self-reliance.
Refugees in urban areas have higher rates of self-reliance than those in camps or settlements, as seen in Chad, Ethiopia, Kenya, and Uganda. Even when refugees have freedom of movement, however, many remain in camps or settlements where economic opportunities are limited. The near-absence of assistance in urban areas may trap destitute refugees in settlements because they lack the financial means to migrate to areas with greater opportunities and cannot afford the risk of moving if they cannot immediately find gainful employment. Moreover, they may not want to leave behind the home and land they have been provided for risk of losing it. Even when camps or settlements are not formally established, the provision of location-based humanitarian assistance—including through the construction of housing and financial support for schools, clinics, and public infrastructure—can lead to a spontaneous process of clustering, which may tie refugees to areas unsuited for economic integration because of skills mismatches, competition for limited resources, or a lack of economic opportunities. If humanitarian assistance were made portable, and refugees could use national health and education services, more refugees would locate in areas where they have greater chances of economic success.

Area-based development may not bring significant gains in self-reliance.
Analysis from Kenya shows that even if encamped refugees were fully economically integrated in the areas where they now live, their incomes would not change significantly, because hosts exhibit significant levels of poverty as well. Refugee camps are found in the more marginal parts of Kenya, with restricted potential for gainful economic activity. The local demand for goods and services is limited because levels of poverty are among the highest in the country and population density is among the lowest. Distances to consumer markets are large and costly to cover, the agropastoral economic potential is constrained by low rainfall and high temperatures, and the potential to develop a (dematerialized, online) service industry is hindered by language barriers and low levels of education of hosts and refugees. Economic development is typically concentrated and unbalanced, and attempts to spread it to remote areas can be costly and ineffective. This is one of the evident shortcomings of the Kalobeyei

experiment, which should provide insights for the area-based development strategies being pursued, including through the Shirika Plan.[2] Area-based development may be justified as a development intervention for hosts, yet area-based development is unlikely to make refugees self-reliant: doing so will require dispersion and freedom of movement to allow refugees to go where the economic opportunities are.

Dismantling large refugee camps requires a considered, gradual approach.
Integrating large refugee populations into the economy overnight would lead to congestion, labor market surplus, overcrowded schools, and additional stresses on health facilities; it would also exacerbate the already dire housing and sanitation conditions that plague many urban and rural areas. In fact, economic activity might even decline if the humanitarian camp economy winds down and the "aid economy" it has created is not replaced by other economic activity, thus leading to reduced demand for local goods and services. Smoothing the outflow of refugees over time can allow the economy to adjust. Governments concerned about large and sudden outflows of refugees to urban areas could set up a permit system in which, each year, a certain number of refugees are given the irrevocable right to move freely around the country in return for the obligation to permanently leave their camp. They could encourage dispersion across the country by shifting development investments to villages welcoming refugees. The assistance model in camps could shift from universal in-kind assistance to portable assistance for those who leave and to employment-based approaches, such as cash for work, for those who remain and are able to work. Refugees who have the capacity to become self-reliant would thus be incentivized to leave and settle elsewhere, and humanitarian assistance could then be targeted to the most vulnerable who cannot work or leave.

Dispersion of refugees requires development investments in host communities. Investing in locations where refugees settle may be essential for durable refugee integration. If conceptualizations of self-reliance fail to adequately consider the implications of refugee inflows on local resources, livelihood opportunities, and public services, the promotion of refugee self-reliance may reduce rather than improve welfare among refugees and hosts. Host areas must provide viable livelihood opportunities for refugees while maintaining hosts' ability to realize their own economic needs and maintain current access levels to essential services, such as education and health. Failure to do so may see local livelihood opportunities and complementary public goods overwhelmed by the presence of refugees, with potentially significant, long-term, negative effects on the livelihoods of refugee and host populations as well as on perceptions of refugee self-reliance models. As such, in many refugee-hosting areas, investments in public goods will be necessary for refugees' integration to be realized.

Preparedness is key to managing refugee inflows effectively and mitigating their impact on host communities. Preparedness is essential because refugees' movements, although often seen as crises, frequently follow predictable patterns. Humanitarian actors already pre-position food and nonfood items close to potential refugee situations, develop rosters of personnel who can be quickly mobilized in response to displacement, and have fundraising systems in place to mobilize funds immediately after a crisis hits. Governments and development partners can similarly take proactive measures, including adjusting rules for fiscal transfers to local governments; preparing public sector deployments in receiving areas; strategically planning refugee accommodations to avoid path dependence and social tensions; and adopting sustainable, inclusive hosting policies. These efforts can ensure a smoother transition for refugees while minimizing the strain on host communities.

Toward Greater Refugee Self-Reliance in SSA

SSA presents a unique paradox in that although most host countries have inclusive policy environments for refugees, low self-reliance remains prevalent among refugees. This report highlights some key, if self-evident, findings. If the ability to work is restricted, refugees will not be able to take care of themselves; when refugees receive tiny pieces of land, they will not be able to live off of it; if assistance is given in certain locations, refugees will flock there; successful economies cannot be built in remote, arid areas; and refugees' dependence implies that aid money has to be spent on care and maintenance and is not available for development. These findings may be self-evident, but they reflect standing practice; combined, they create an environment in which self-reliance is inhibited and dependence thrives.

A successful transformation toward self-reliance implies deep changes to the prevailing refugee-hosting model. Refugees' economic participation will need to strengthen and their aid dependency decrease, whereas reliance on encampment will have to be reduced and inclusion in public service provision promoted. The way refugee situations are financed will also have to change, with less reliance on humanitarian assistance and a greater role for development assistance that places more emphasis on multiyear predictable financing and on financing modalities that reflect the nature of spending, such as investments in development projects, budget support, and results-based financing for recurrent spending. Because refugees' economic inclusion can lead to friction with hosts, refugee policies will need to carefully consider and address the concerns of host governments and invest in the economic development of refugee *and* host populations. Such an approach is summarized in figure ES.4.

Figure ES.4   Key Elements to Promoting Refugee Self-Reliance

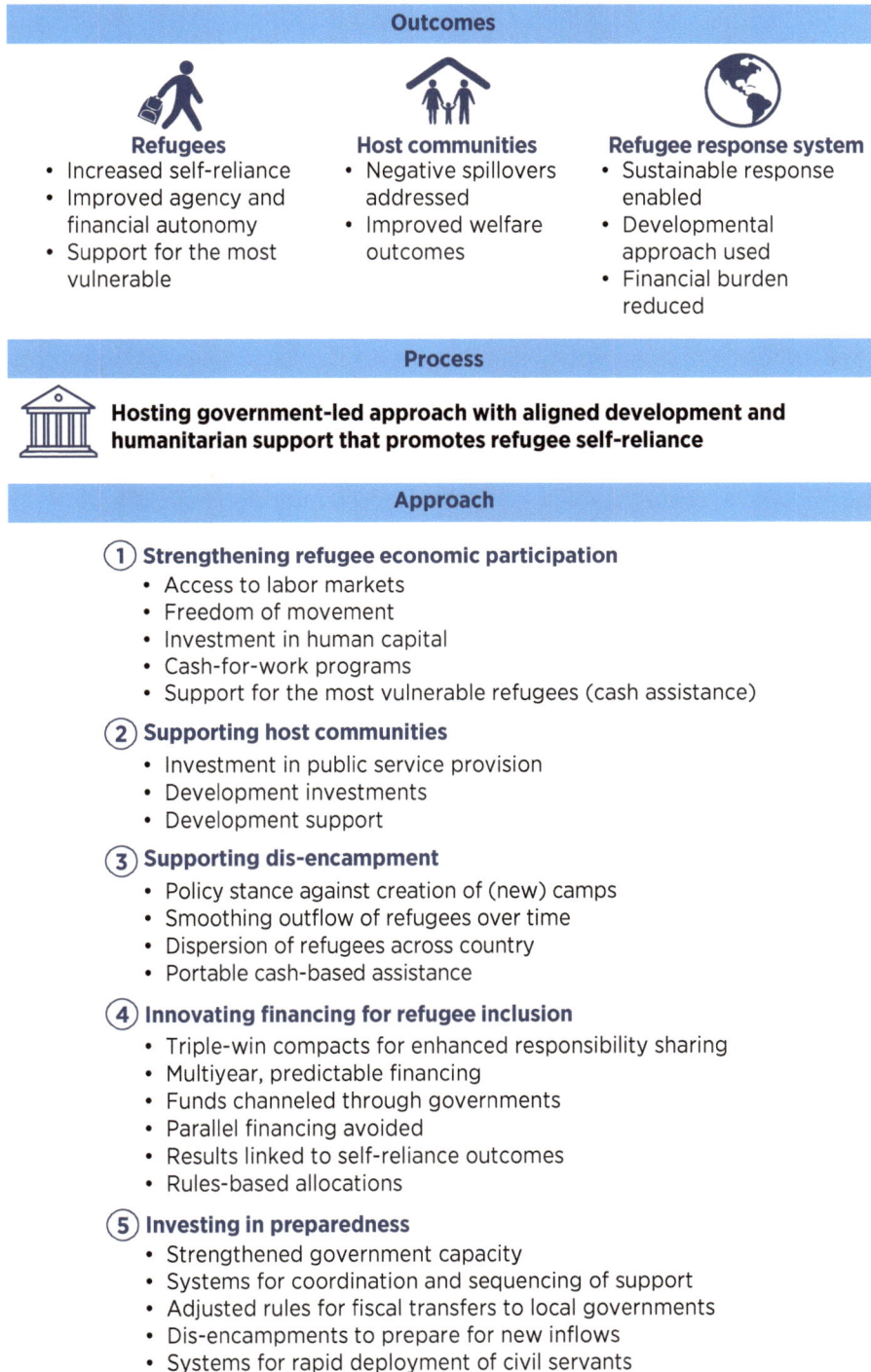

Outcomes

Refugees
- Increased self-reliance
- Improved agency and financial autonomy
- Support for the most vulnerable

Host communities
- Negative spillovers addressed
- Improved welfare outcomes

Refugee response system
- Sustainable response enabled
- Developmental approach used
- Financial burden reduced

Process

Hosting government-led approach with aligned development and humanitarian support that promotes refugee self-reliance

Approach

(1) Strengthening refugee economic participation
- Access to labor markets
- Freedom of movement
- Investment in human capital
- Cash-for-work programs
- Support for the most vulnerable refugees (cash assistance)

(2) Supporting host communities
- Investment in public service provision
- Development investments
- Development support

(3) Supporting dis-encampment
- Policy stance against creation of (new) camps
- Smoothing outflow of refugees over time
- Dispersion of refugees across country
- Portable cash-based assistance

(4) Innovating financing for refugee inclusion
- Triple-win compacts for enhanced responsibility sharing
- Multiyear, predictable financing
- Funds channeled through governments
- Parallel financing avoided
- Results linked to self-reliance outcomes
- Rules-based allocations

(5) Investing in preparedness
- Strengthened government capacity
- Systems for coordination and sequencing of support
- Adjusted rules for fiscal transfers to local governments
- Dis-encampments to prepare for new inflows
- Systems for rapid deployment of civil servants

Source: Original figure created for this report.

What is required is a shift in perspective away from considering refugees as a burden to one that emphasizes the scope for local development and a triple win—that is, with benefits for host countries, refugees, and the international community alike. Refugees have agency, abilities, and a revealed preference for financial autonomy and self-reliance. When refugees are more economically active, assistance for their care and maintenance can be reduced. Resources spent on handouts for refugees who are capable and ready to take care of themselves can be invested more productively in strengthening refugees' productive capacity and restoring their asset base, providing social assistance to vulnerable refugees who are unable to work, and promoting the growth and development of host economies. If refugees are able to go to schools and clinics used by nationals, they have less reason to remain in camps, where parallel systems are the norm, and investments could be redirected to strengthening national schools, clinics, and systems. In this way, a triple win is created—one whereby refugees have jobs, savings on humanitarian aid are realized, and investments are made in the economic development of host countries.

The spending that could be reallocated toward development is significant. A 25 percent increase in refugees' incomes in SSA would unlock an additional $900 million per year for investments in development, assuming financial commitments from donors remain unchanged. These resources could be allocated to support the most vulnerable refugees, or they could be channeled to host governments and used to address negative distributional effects and to invest in job creation and economic opportunities for refugees and host communities alike.

A shift to greater economic inclusion by host countries should be accompanied by predictable, rules-based developmental financing that uses government systems and favors economic inclusion over needs. Refugee financing will have to become "incentive compatible" and less based on needs. Needs will always be higher when refugees have few economic opportunities, and financing that reflects needs not only is costly but also effectively rewards economic exclusion. Instead, financing should reward countries for shrinking the financial burden of hosting refugees by including them in their economies. Refugees' inclusion necessitates investing in their productive capacity and addressing negative spillovers of inclusion. It also requires investments to meet the recurrent expenditures for national education and health service delivery and system strengthening. Host countries are more likely to implement inclusive policies with the assurance of multiyear financing that is results based and channeled through the treasury. Parallel financing, including paid-for services, is to be avoided.

A rules-based allocation system determined on the scale of the challenge, host governments' financial capacity, and the sustainability of country responses could be used to allocate funds. Such a system could take into account aspects such as the wealth of a country (less need for financial burden sharing with higher-income countries); the number of refugees; the protractedness of the situation (emergency situations are expensive); the prevailing refugee policy framework; and the inclusion of refugees in national economies with, possibly, separate windows for host governments and humanitarian agencies. IDA allocations are determined using such a formula-based approach, and refugee financing could take its cue from this approach.

Host governments must take leadership of the refugee response. Once an inclusive policy environment is in place, governments can take a strong policy stance against encampment, work with humanitarian partners on dis-encampment strategies, or establish clear transition plans for temporary camps where necessary. They can advocate for triple-win compacts to unlock development financing that can be invested in economic development, expand national public service provision, and address any negative spillovers from inclusion. They can clearly demarcate the roles and responsibilities of partners that operate within their borders to prevent redundancies in service delivery while strengthening national systems.

Like many reforms across sectors, moving from parallel systems to refugees' inclusion introduces changes to the status quo, including shifts in roles and responsibilities. These changes can create opportunities for improved collaboration and partnerships between government and humanitarian actors. However, inclusion inevitably means reducing the role of actors involved in parallel systems, including those of humanitarian actors and specialized refugee agencies, and increasing the responsibilities of relevant line ministries and government agencies. These shifts need to be managed carefully to mitigate risks around perceived competition over resources and policy influence.

Humanitarian agencies must adapt their roles to support long-term development, reduce redundancy in service delivery, and enhance the efficiency of humanitarian aid. Often stretched thin, humanitarian agencies face challenges in balancing their emergency response and legal protection mandates with refugees' long-term development needs. As refugees increasingly access national health and education systems, the necessity of parallel humanitarian services diminishes. Although humanitarian agencies may still provide specialized services addressing refugees' unique vulnerabilities, such as legal protection or return assistance, a focus on the "core" business and a shift to national systems are essential.

Significant opportunity exists to align development financing (including financing from the Window for Host Communities and Refugees) with efforts to avoid encampment and promote self-reliance. Nearly all encamped refugees (99.8 percent) are found in IDA or IDA-blend countries, suggesting that, in these countries, development financing can be leveraged to promote self-reliance and invest in jobs for refugees as well as hosts. Money currently spent on subsistence needs can be more productively invested in service quality, jobs, and economic development in host communities, or it can be reallocated to host governments to support the recurrent spending they incur from including refugees in national services.

Notes

1. Unless otherwise indicated, poverty is measured by the international poverty line of PPP$ 2.15 for low-income countries, and by the global poverty line of PPP$ 3.65 for lower-middle-income countries. PPP = purchasing power parity.
2. The Kalobeyei experiment and the Shirika Plan are refugee response strategies adopted by the government of Kenya to promote refugee socioeconomic inclusion within integrated settlements, accompanied by investments in area-based development.

References

Hoogeveen, J., and R. B. Hopper. 2024. "Using Poverty Lines to Measure Refugee Self-Reliance." Policy Research Working Paper 10910, World Bank, Washington, DC.

KNBS (Kenya National Bureau of Statistics). 2024. *Poverty Report: Based on the 2022 Kenya Continuous Household Survey*. Nairobi: KNBS.

Abbreviations

FDP	forcibly displaced person
ha	hectare
IDA	International Development Association
IDP	internally displaced person
IPL	international poverty line
km	kilometer
LIC	low-income country
LMIC	lower-middle-income country
PPP	purchasing power parity
PWP	public works program
SSA	Sub-Saharan Africa
UMIC	upper-middle-income country

All dollars are US dollars unless otherwise indicated.

PART I

Setting the Context

CHAPTER 1

Generously Hosting Refugees in a Way That Creates Dependency

On the Need to Reform the Approach to Hosting Refugees

Sub-Saharan Africa (SSA) hosts some of the world's largest and most protracted refugee situations. Across the region, millions have been forced to seek safety in neighboring countries that often struggle to provide adequate resources to meet their own, let alone refugees', needs. The conflict that erupted in Sudan in April 2023, which resulted in one of the largest and fastest-growing displacement crises in recent history, exemplifies these challenges. Over 12 million people have been forced to flee their homes to date, with more than 2 million seeking refuge in neighboring countries such as Chad, which as of January 2025 hosted 740,000 newly arrived refugees and asylum seekers from Sudan. The continuous influx of people has created a situation in which refugees outnumber local populations in some areas, with inevitable consequences for social cohesion and economic and political stability.

The refugee situation in Chad illustrates some of the challenges the global refugee response system is operating under as a result of two concurrent developments. First, the global refugee population under the mandate of the UN Refugee Agency (UNHCR) increased by one-third in two and a half years, from 21.3 million refugees in 2021 to almost 32.0 million by mid-2024 (figure 1.1, panel a). Of this population, 9 million, or 28 percent of refugees globally, live in SSA (UNHCR 2024). More than two-thirds (69 percent) of refugees in SSA came from just five countries: the Central African Republic, the Democratic Republic of Congo, Somalia, South Sudan, and Sudan. Most fleeing conflict seek safety in the nearest possible location, either within their own country or within neighboring countries.[1] Consequently, most refugees are hosted by a small number of countries. Over one-half reside in just four countries—Uganda, Chad, Ethiopia, and Sudan—and nearly 90 percent are hosted by just 10 countries

Figure 1.1   Refugee Trends and Top-10 Refugee-Hosting Countries in SSA

a. Number of refugees,
SSA and globally, 2010–24

b. Number of refugees 10
SSA countries, 2024

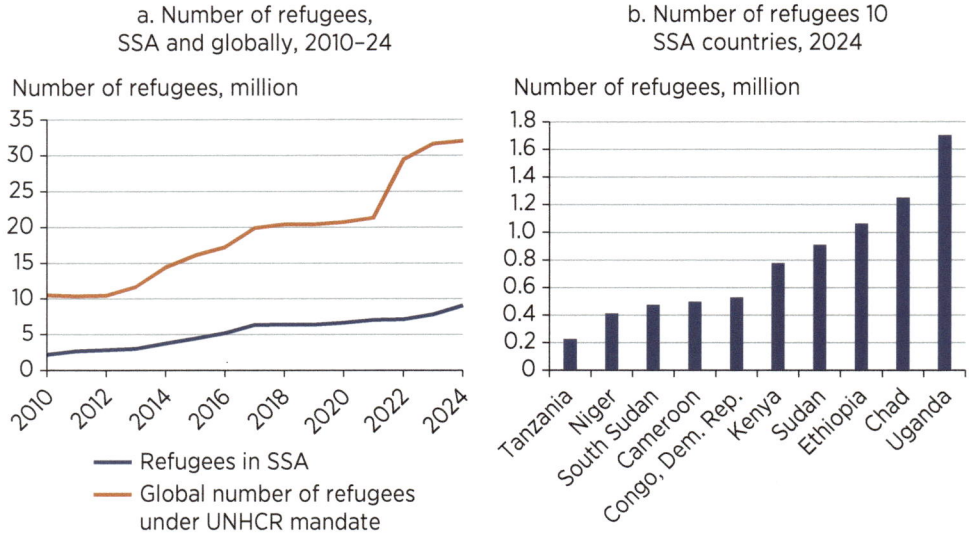

Source: Original calculations based on UNHCR Refugee Data Finder (accessed September 25, 2024).

Note: In panel a, the significant increase in 2022 reflects the 5.7 million people who fled Ukraine and the 4.4 million other nationalities, primarily Afghans and Venezuelans, who also fled their countries (UNHCR 2023). SSA = Sub-Saharan Africa; UNHCR = UN Refugee Agency.

(figure 1.1, panel b). Second, the amount of humanitarian financing available to address these challenges in low- and middle-income countries has remained largely unchanged, constraining the amount available per refugee (figure 1.2, panel b).

Rooted in the human readiness to assist those in need, the provision of protection to refugees is mandated by international law. Its effective provision necessitates collective action by all nations.[2] The international community is committed to such action, as confirmed recently by the 2018 Global Compact on Refugees, in which international donors, humanitarian agencies, and refugee-hosting countries agreed to equitable burden and responsibility sharing to ease pressures on countries hosting refugees. At the same time, situations like the Chad emergency raise doubts about the sustainability of these approaches, which keep refugees reliant on humanitarian aid. Concerns include the lack of long-term prospects for refugees, the extent of deprivation they experience, and its detrimental effects on their well-being. These concerns prompt questions about whether funds spent every year on

Figure 1.2   Changes in Composition of ODA Provided by OECD Countries, 2018–21

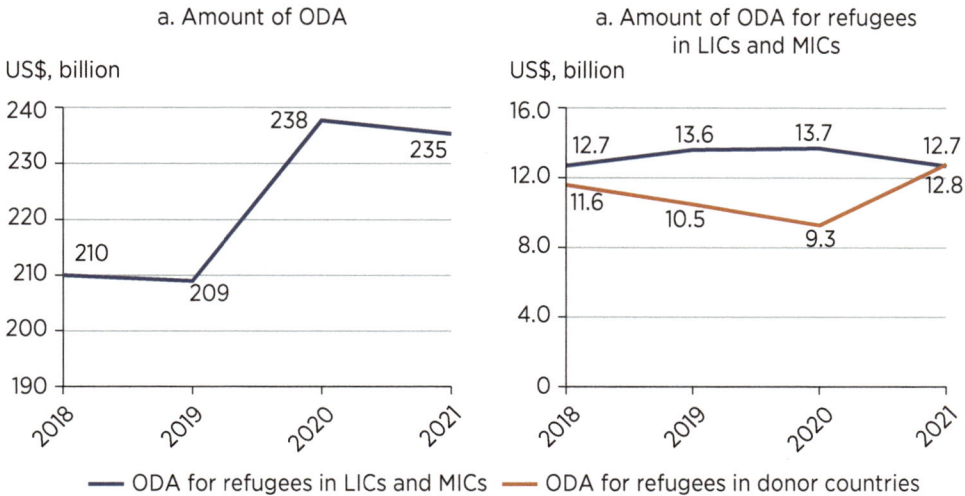

a. Amount of ODA

US$, billion

a. Amount of ODA for refugees in LICs and MICs

US$, billion

— ODA for refugees in LICs and MICs   — ODA for refugees in donor countries

Source: OECD 2023.

Note: LIC = low-income country; MIC = middle-income country; ODA = official development assistance; OECD = Organisation for Economic Co-operation and Development.

humanitarian assistance could instead be invested in more durable solutions that benefit both hosts and refugees. Additionally, uncertainty prevails about whether resources will continue to be available to support refugee hosting, especially because their numbers will very likely continue rising, and as new policy priorities place increasing claims on development financing (World Bank 2023a).

There is thus an urgent need to adjust how humanitarian partners, developmental actors, and host governments respond to refugee situations. Although advocacy for additional financing remains important, the immediate challenge is to strengthen the efficiency and effectiveness of existing responses. Most notably, a departure from the established care and maintenance model of humanitarian support toward a more sustainable approach, focused on economic inclusion and the promotion of self-reliance, is much needed.

UNHCR launched the "Sustainable Responses" effort in 2024 to refocus its engagement model toward a more inclusive and durable model of support.

Sustainable Responses is about maximizing self-reliance and minimizing dependence on humanitarian aid by expanding the human potential of forcibly displaced people and supporting host governments to bring refugees into their national systems (UNHCR 2025). At least three distinct advantages are associated with increasing the self-reliance of refugees: (1) it reduces dependence on humanitarian assistance and improves the dignity and financial autonomy of refugees; (2) increased earnings by refugees themselves mean that less humanitarian assistance is needed, so this assistance can be steered to the most vulnerable; and (3) the savings on humanitarian assistance realized by promoting refugee self-reliance can be allocated to development interventions that support hosts and refugees. By accelerating economic development, these interventions can create an environment conducive to refugees' economic inclusion and the development of host regions.

Most countries in SSA already embrace self-reliance as the preferred approach to hosting refugees and have taken significant steps in this direction. These steps include closing camps and implementing inclusive policies, such as integrating refugee children into public schools and granting access to land and labor markets. Despite these efforts, the results have been underwhelming. This lack of success highlights the need to systematically document countries' experiences in promoting self-reliance and to identify factors that have thus far made refugee self-reliance largely elusive.

A successful transformation toward self-reliance implies changes to the prevailing refugee-hosting model. Reliance on encampment must be reduced and inclusion in public service provision promoted. The way refugee situations are financed has to change. One envisions less reliance on humanitarian assistance and a greater role for development assistance that is channeled through host government systems, with more emphasis on multiyear, predictable financing, and on financing modalities that reflect the nature of spending (investment project financing for investments, budget support and results-based financing for recurrent spending). Furthermore, as refugees' economic inclusion potentially leads to friction with hosts, refugee policies can be expected to increasingly focus on both refugee and host populations.

These reforms will be relevant and profound for host countries across the globe, but especially so in Africa, where the approach based on care and maintenance camps is far more ubiquitous than in Europe and Central Asia, Latin America and the Caribbean, or the Middle East and North Africa (figure 1.3).

Figure 1.3   Percent of Refugees Living in Camps or Camp-Like Situations, Selected Regions

Percent

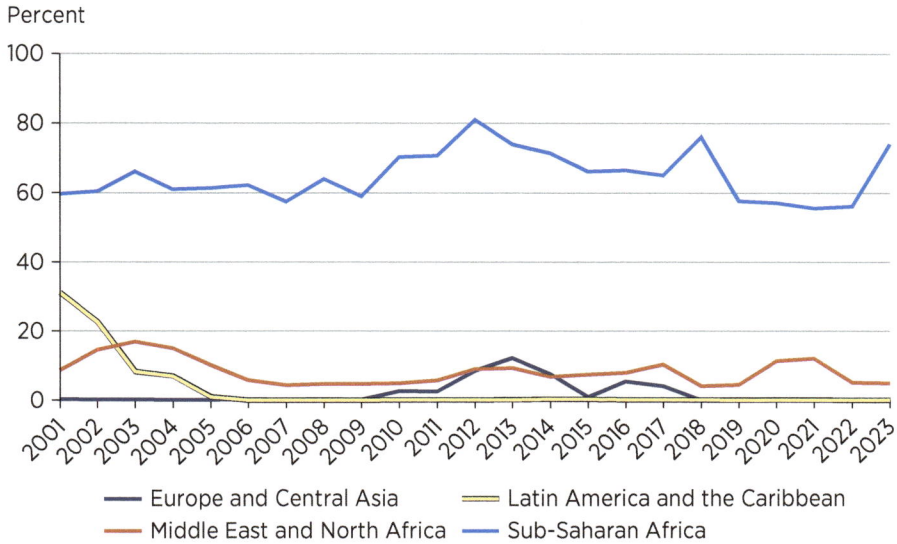

Source: Original calculations using data from the United Nations High Commissioner for Refugees' Global Data Service.

Refugees in SSA

Forced displacement has profound adverse effects on well-being. The threat or realization of violence, persecution, and conflict often leads refugees to flee their homes abruptly and forces them to leave behind assets and livelihoods as well as family and sociocultural ties to undertake dangerous journeys in the pursuit of safety. Because refugees prioritize safety, they frequently find themselves in places with limited livelihood opportunities and services, or where their skills do not match the local economy. Consequently, conflict and displacement are important drivers of extremely elevated levels of poverty and destitution. Even before households are forced to flee, conflict and violence inflict significant economic costs. Agricultural production declines, land and property values depreciate, and government services and assistance are frequently disrupted. In situations of violent conflict, property may be destroyed, seized, or stolen. People fleeing conflict are forced to abandon their land, homes, and unharvested crops as well as leave behind assets that cannot be liquidated or transported easily. They may be forced to use their savings or to borrow to pay for the cost of their journey. The loss of these assets significantly diminishes refugees' capacity to cope with their changed circumstances and to meet their own basic needs.

The disruptions to health, education, and services in conflict-affected places of origin often have adverse effects on refugees' human capital. For instance, refugees often experience high prevalence rates of various health conditions due to the impact of conflict on health care services in their home countries, the conditions of their displacement, and food insecurity in both their places of origin and host communities.[3] Education is frequently disrupted in conflict situations and during flight, with adverse consequences for human capital, constraining refugees' future opportunities to find secure employment, earn higher incomes, and become self-reliant.

Forced displacement often leads to the dislocation of households from their extended families and communities, bringing a loss of social capital, which can be a source of transfers in cash or in in-kind assistance in the event of a future shock, as well as providing physical or emotional support in crises. Social capital can also play an important role in matching jobseekers to employers, particularly in informal labor markets.

Over the last decade in SSA, an average of 4 percent of refugees per year returned to their countries of origin, whereas less than 1 percent per year resettled in third countries, with only a handful naturalized (figure 1.4).[4] The lack of durable solutions for refugees has contributed to the growing number of displaced persons in the region, because new refugee flows outpace durable solutions and increasing numbers of refugees find themselves in protracted situations, with nearly 66 percent displaced for five consecutive years or more (UNHCR 2023).

Figure 1.4   Percent of Refugees in SSA Achieving Durable Solutions, 2014–23

Percent of refugees

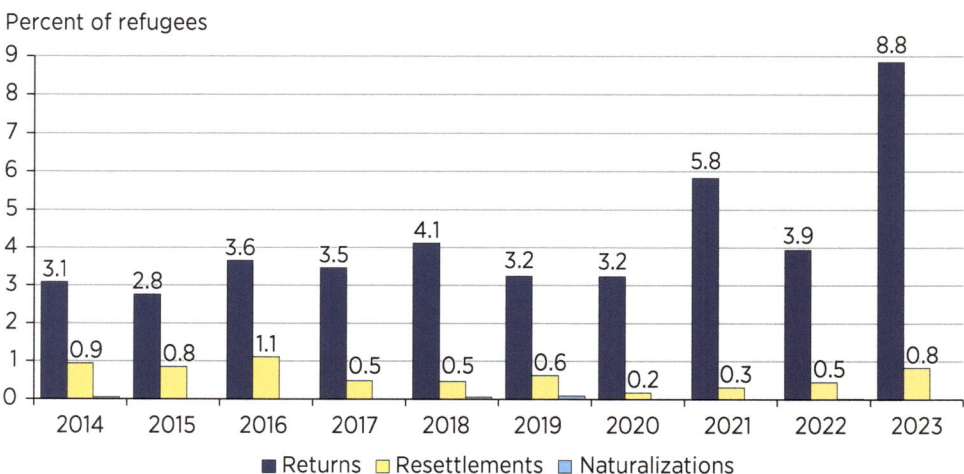

Source: Sarzin and Nsababera 2024.

Refugees in SSA are dominated by dependents, with the region hosting the highest proportion of children (54 percent), the lowest proportion of working-age men (19 percent), and the lowest proportion of working-age adults (42 percent) among its refugee population (figure 1.5).[5] The very high proportion of women and children (77 percent) makes the refugee population in SSA more vulnerable to protection risks and amplifies demand for education and health services. Concurrently, the high proportion of children and low proportion of working-age adults imply high dependency ratios, posing significant obstacles to fostering refugee self-reliance in the region. Harmonized data from Chad, Ethiopia, Niger, and Uganda reveal the proportion of women-headed households among the refugee population to be twice as high as among the host population: 50 percent for refugee households compared to 26 percent for hosts, with these households typically facing higher rates of poverty and increased vulnerability (Jarotschkin et al. 2023; Nguyen, Savadogo, and Tanaka 2021; World Bank 2019).

Figure 1.5   Decomposition of Refugee Population, by Age and World Region

Percent

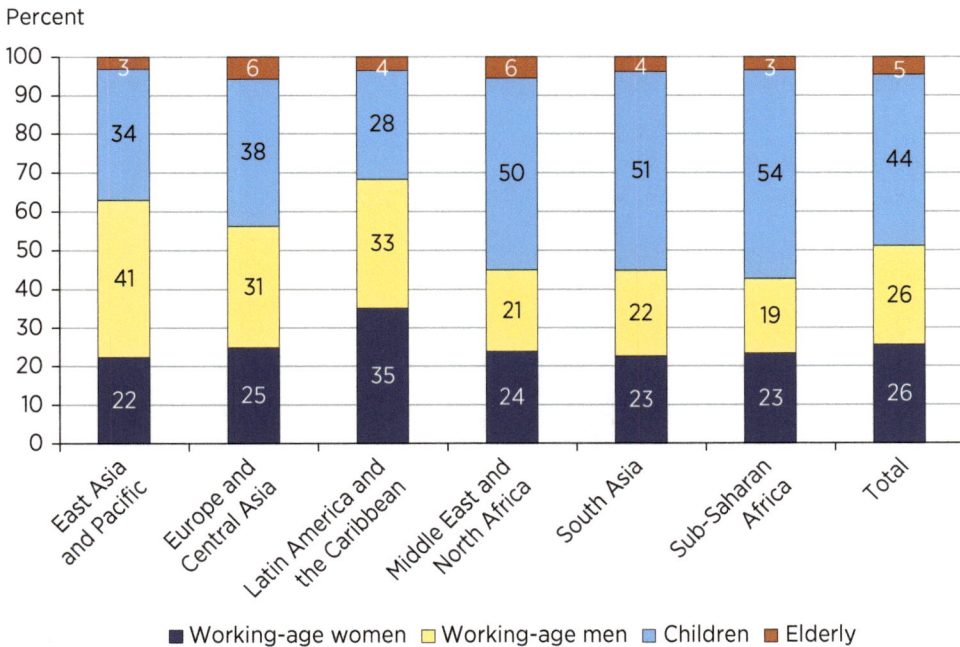

■ Working-age women □ Working-age men □ Children ■ Elderly

Source: Sarzin and Nsababera 2024.

Refugees in SSA also frequently settle in remote and marginalized border regions in neighboring countries; these regions typically have limited economic opportunities but may allow for cross-border movements, and refugees often share ethnic identities, languages, or social ties with host communities there (Vancluysen 2022). The concentration of refugees in rural areas is also an outcome of the deliberate policies of many host governments to settle refugees in government-designated sites, often in remote areas (Kibreab 2007). Host governments may pursue such policies to minimize an actual or perceived risk to national security; deter the integration of refugees into host societies; prevent refugees from competing with nationals for employment, resources, and services; or limit changes in ethnic balances. According to available UNHCR data, SSA is the region with the smallest proportion of refugees in urban areas (9 percent), a proportion that has remained relatively constant over the last decade (figure 1.6).[6] The presence of refugees in areas with limited economic opportunities, inadequate infrastructure, and already poor access to services poses significant challenges to fostering refugees' self-reliance and supporting their inclusion in national service delivery systems.

Figure 1.6   Location of Refugees, by World Region

Percent of refugees

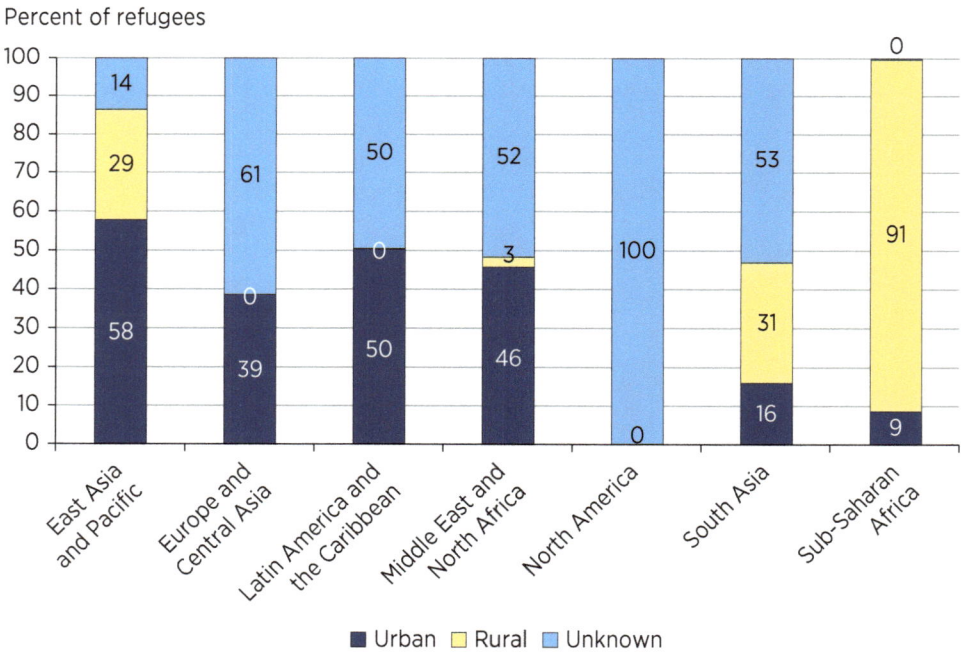

Source: Sarzin and Nsababera 2024.

A large proportion of refugees in SSA is confined to camps and formal or informal settlements, limiting opportunities for self-reliance. In many SSA countries, encampment policies are coupled with movement restrictions, reducing income-earning opportunities and increasing dependence on aid. Aid dependency is thus high among refugees (Jarotschkin et al. 2023; Pape, Petrini, and Iqbal 2018; World Bank 2019). Harmonized survey data from Chad, Ethiopia, Niger, and Uganda show that employment rates for refugees are lower than for hosts— 56 percent of adult male refugees are employed compared to 80 percent of hosts. Employment rates for adult female refugees are even lower: only 35 percent compared to 55 percent of female hosts (World Bank 2023a).

Refugees who do work are often employed as casual laborers or are engaged in nonfarm self-employment, typically in small trade or services, or as incentive workers by international organizations (Jarotschkin et al. 2023; Nguyen, Savadogo, and Tanaka 2021; Pape, Petrini, and Iqbal 2018; World Bank 2019). Refugees in wage employment are frequently paid less than nationals and face discrimination in the workplace (Nguyen, Savadogo, and Tanaka 2021; World Bank 2019). Many refugees in SSA have agricultural backgrounds but limited access to land, resulting in a lower proportion of refugees engaged in own-account agriculture compared to hosts (Jarotschkin et al. 2023; Nguyen, Savadogo, and Tanaka 2021; Pape, Petrini, and Iqbal 2018). When refugees are able to cultivate land, their cultivation contributes only a modest share of household income because refugees, on average, have comparatively smaller plots than hosts and use fewer agricultural inputs and productive tools (Nguyen, Savadogo, and Tanaka 2021).

Refugees in camps and settlements, by contrast, often have better access and proximity to social services compared to host communities, reflecting the significant humanitarian response in refugee camps. For instance, refugees in Chad have better access to education, health care, and improved sanitation and water sources compared to host communities (Nguyen, Savadogo, and Tanaka 2021). Similarly, in Ethiopia, refugees enjoy comparable or better access to basic services than hosts (Pape, Petrini, and Iqbal 2018). In Uganda, refugee households have better access to electricity and improved sanitation and water; outside Kampala, health care centers are slightly more accessible to refugees than hosts, both financially and in terms of geographical proximity (World Bank 2019). In Niger, refugee households also have better access to improved water (World Bank 2023b).

Despite preferable access to humanitarian services, lack of rights to socioeconomic opportunities can prevent refugees from overcoming their displacement-related vulnerabilities and rebuilding their lives. In addition to the right to freedom of movement, refugees' rights to employment and national services play a critical role in explaining the variation in their socioeconomic outcomes across host countries. Africa has been at the forefront of establishing a regional legal framework governing protection of and assistance to refugees and internally displaced persons. The 1969 Organisation of African Unity Convention was the first regional instrument on refugees (inspiring development of the 1984 Cartagena Declaration in Latin America). It introduced several important innovations in international law and remains the only legally binding regional instrument on refugees. The 2009 Kampala Convention—the first and only legally binding instrument on internal displacement globally—provides a comprehensive legal framework for addressing internal displacement in Africa.

Many SSA countries have domesticated the provisions of the Organisation of African Unity Convention and the Kampala Convention into their national laws, providing broad de jure rights to refugees; however, access to socioeconomic opportunities remains limited, leaving a gap between refugees' de jure rights and the de facto realization of those rights (figure 1.7). A 2021 global survey of refugees' work rights found that 11 SSA countries, which together host more than

Figure 1.7   Refugees' Work Rights in Law and in Practice, Selected Sub-Saharan African Countries

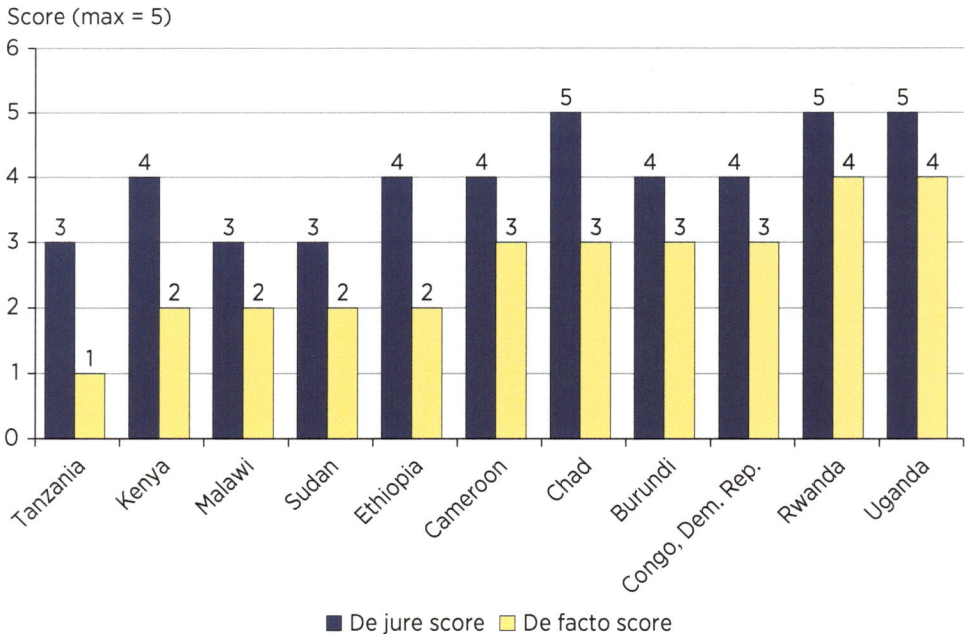

Score (max = 5)

■ De jure score   □ De facto score

Source: Sarzin and Nsababera 2024.

Note: De jure work rights are scored on a 5-point scale: 1 = existing national policies prohibit refugees from working, and 5 = fully functioning national policies support refugees' right to work without restrictions and extend labor protections to refugees. Similarly, de facto work rights are scored on a 5-point scale based on the actualization of rights across five areas: right to wage employment, right to self-employment, freedom to travel domestically, freedom to choose a place of residence, and rights at work (Ginn et al. 2022).

80 percent of the region's refugee population, perform moderately well in terms of de jure work rights for refugees, with 8 out of the 11 countries receiving a score of 4 or 5 on a five-point scale of workers' rights. Only two countries, however, received a de facto ("in practice") score of 4 for labor market access, and none scored 5. All other countries scored 3 or below on de facto access, indicating restrictive practices. Tanzania received the lowest score because of its restrictive policies, which include crackdowns on work, even within camps (Ginn et al. 2022).

In many SSA countries, refugees have access to primary education and health services close to or on par with that of host communities (figure 1.8). At secondary and tertiary levels of education, however, refugees have poorer access. Of the 11 SSA countries surveyed for the 2022 Global Refugee Work Rights Report (Ginn et al. 2022), 10 obtained a score of 4 or 5 (on a five-point scale) for de facto access to primary education and 8 obtained a score of 4 or 5 for de facto access to secondary education. On access to tertiary education, however, only Cameroon and Rwanda obtained a score of 4 or 5. In terms of access to health services, 8 out of 11 surveyed SSA countries obtained a score of 4 or 5 (on a five-point scale) for de facto access to health services. In three countries (the Democratic Republic of Congo, Sudan, and Tanzania), refugees face difficulties in accessing health services, with scores of 3 or lower.

Figure 1.8   Refugees' Access to Education and Health Care, Selected Sub-Saharan African Countries

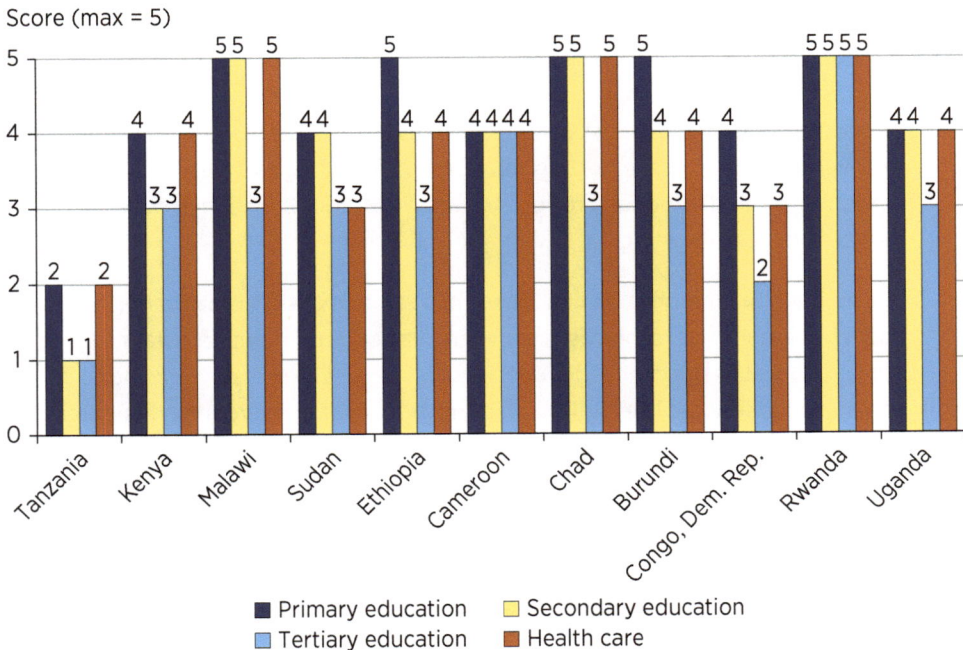

Source: Sarzin and Nsababera 2024.

Making Refugee Self-Reliance Work

The current refugee response model is under immense strain. The prevailing approach—which relies heavily on short-term humanitarian interventions— fosters dependence and limits self-sufficiency, preventing the system from delivering sustainable outcomes for refugees. By contrast, enabling refugees to earn higher incomes would enhance their financial autonomy while reducing their reliance on humanitarian assistance. Similarly, integrating refugees into national schools and health care systems, rather than maintaining parallel structures, could help bridge disparities in education and health while generating cost savings. These savings could be reinvested in broader development efforts in host countries. By shifting to a more sustainable approach, a triple win can emerge, benefiting refugees, humanitarian agencies, and host communities alike. This report explores how such a transformation can be achieved.

At the heart of this report is the recognition that the current refugee-hosting approach is inefficient. The approach allocates substantial resources to care and maintenance for refugees who are both capable and willing to support themselves. Instead, this report proposes a different way, one in which the resources presently spent on consumables are invested in the growth and development of host economies.

How might a self-reliance approach work? Because of the cost for supporting refugees, the availability of adequate external financing is key to success; however, the cost of hosting refugees is also a function of host countries' policies. For example, it is of course more expensive to sustain refugees through assistance programs than it is to let them work and earn a living. A sustainable response model to refugee situations requires (1) predictable external financing to cover the fiscal costs of hosting refugees, (2) financing to invest in host communities' and refugees' productive capacities, and (3) effective policies to reduce the cost of hosting.

In the short run, during the initial phase of a refugee crisis, humanitarian agencies remain first responders, providing critical emergency assistance to new arrivals, while it is upon host governments to allow refugees to work and to access public services like health and education. As the emergency dissipates and refugees begin to earn income, their earnings, if sufficient, will make it feasible to reduce the amount of aid needed for consumption support, although financing to cover the cost of health and education provision will remain critical at this early stage. Donors can reallocate the savings on humanitarian assistance to invest in host communities and to restore refugees' productive capacities, thus laying the foundation for a virtuous cycle and even greater savings in the future.

In the medium term, when the economy has adapted, and when refugees have become more financially autonomous, donors can realign their financial support to other development priorities.

What this approach sketches is a refugee hosting model that costs less, thereby allowing for increased investment in growth and economic development. Making such a solution a reality will require addressing several key challenges. Host country concerns—often around the potential for conflict with local populations—must be managed, and the financing model for hosting refugees needs to be restructured. Funds previously allocated to humanitarian actors need to be directed through host governments to offset the additional costs of providing health, education, and social protection services to refugees. Meanwhile, development actors must work with host governments to invest in improving service quality, expanding job opportunities, and fostering economic development in host communities.

When it comes to refugees, scale matters. It is one thing to close Avepozo camp, which housed just 800 refugees near the capital city of Togo, Lomé (Avepozo was closed in 2022). It is many times more challenging to close Kakuma camp, home to almost 300,000 people who live in an arid and isolated corner of Kenya. As refugee situations involve more people, political concerns increase about the possible consequences for host populations, potential security challenges, or ethnic balance. Responding in a sustainable way requires identifying these concerns and addressing them appropriately.

Comprehensive ways to deal with large refugee numbers, whether originating from a crisis or from dis-encampment, need to be developed. Doing so successfully will likely require a set of complementary actions, including identifying ways to smooth the flow of refugees over time and to disperse refugees spatially, all while recognizing the importance of free movement and of incentivizing communities to host refugees. Smoothing may require temporary encampment, area-based development around existing camps, or large-scale public works programs that are reduced over time. Dispersion may require incentivizing refugees to relocate across the host country and offering benefits to locations that receive refugees. These strategies can be strengthened through emergency preparedness. Although refugee inflows are often seen as crises, many large movements can be forecast through an assessment of the sociopolitical situation in neighboring countries and early cross-border movements. Emergency preparedness can strengthen the efficiency and cost-effectiveness of hosting refugees in the initial phase of a crisis.

Above all, a fundamental shift in mindset is needed—one that moves beyond seeing refugees solely as vulnerable individuals in need of assistance and instead recognizes them as people with agency, resilience, and the potential to rebuild their lives if given the right support. This mindset must reject quick fixes, such as the creation of large camps, and focus instead on practical, government-led, sustainable solutions. It should prioritize meaningful engagement with host communities and their representatives in government, and work with these groups to realize durable solutions that benefit both refugees and hosts, ensuring long-term stability and shared prosperity.

About This Report

The objectives of this report are threefold: (1) to understand the factors that support or hinder refugee self-reliance; (2) to investigate opportunities for a more sustainable refugee response system; and (3) to identify policy actions that make the transition to a more efficient way of hosting refugees feasible. To achieve these aims, this report begins by clarifying what is meant by refugee self-reliance and exploring the factors that constrain it. It then identifies potential efficiency gains from increasing self-reliance and quantifies the cost savings that could be realized by moving away from the current care and maintenance model of assistance. If these savings are reinvested to address barriers to self-reliance, the refugee-hosting system can shift from simply "giving people fish" to "allowing people to fish" or, in development terms, from a humanitarian approach to a development one.

The report is organized in three parts. After this first part, which sets the context, part II clarifies the definition and measurement of self-reliance and then applies the new proposed measure in two ways. First, it explores empirically the degree of self-reliance in SSA. Building on the fact that self-reliance reduces the cost of humanitarian assistance, it next estimates by how much the cost for refugees' care and maintenance could be reduced with increased self-reliance. These savings form the basis for a potential grand bargain in which increased refugee self-reliance frees up resources that can be invested in the most vulnerable refugees and the economic development of the hosting nation, to the betterment of hosts and refugees alike.

Part III presents four country case studies. Vignettes from Chad, Kenya, Niger, and Uganda—countries that have made strides in promoting refugee self-reliance, remain committed to advancing it, but face ongoing challenges in realizing its full potential—provide insight into factors that constrain self-reliance. The last chapter draws lessons from these countries and proposes approaches focused on facilitating a transition away from a care and maintenance approach toward increased refugee integration. Approaches include recommendations focused on host government leadership, better preparedness, increased development investments, the spatial dispersion of refugees, and the smoothing of refugee flows across a country over time. The chapter finally explores what changes in the global financial architecture are needed to better align host governments' incentives with increased self-reliance and how current approaches to refugee crises can be altered to facilitate refugee self-reliance and improve outcomes for hosts and refugees alike.

Notes

1. Distance between origin and destination countries is the single most important determinant of dyadic refugee flows (Echevarria and Gardeazabal 2016; Iqbal 2007).
2. Per the 1951 Convention Relating to the Status of Refugees (also referred to as the 1951 Geneva Convention), a refugee is a person who is outside the country of his/her nationality and is unable or, owing to a "well-founded fear" of being persecuted, unwilling to return and avail themselves of the protection of that country. The 1951 Geneva Convention also highlights the need for collective action by observing that "the grant of asylum may place unduly heavy burdens on certain countries, and that a satisfactory solution of a problem of which the United Nations has recognized the international scope and nature cannot therefore be achieved without international co-operation."
3. Baauw et al. (2019) found high rates of a range of health conditions among refugee children arriving in Australia, Canada, Germany, Malta, the Netherlands, New Zealand, Spain, the United Kingdom, and the United States.
4. Over the last decade, less than 16,000 refugees in SSA were naturalized in countries of asylum. Only one case of large-scale naturalization exists in the region—the naturalization of almost 150,000 former Burundian refugees in Tanzania in 2009.
5. The low proportion of refugee men in many host countries is likely due to several factors, including men remaining in countries of origin to fight or protect property, higher fatality rates for men in conflict, and men engaging in more dangerous secondary movements outside the region. Calculations are based on UNHCR data, which cover almost all registered refugees in SSA (94 percent) and the Middle East and North Africa (98 percent), but incomplete data for other regions make regional comparisons difficult.
6. UNHCR data on the location of refugees in SSA are complete only from 2010 onward.

References

Baauw, Albertine, Joana Kist-van Holthe, Bridget Slattery, Martijn Heymans, Mai Chinapaw, and Hans van Goudoever. 2019. "Health Needs of Refugee Children Identified on Arrival in Reception Countries: A Systematic Review and Meta-Analysis." *BMJ Pediatrics Open* 3 (1): e000516. https://doi.org/10.1136/bmjpo-2019-000516.

Echevarria, Jon, and Javier Gardeazabal. 2016. "Refugee Gravitation." *Public Choice* 169 (3): 269–92.

Ginn, Thomas, Reva Resstack, Helen Dempster, Emily Arnold-Fernández, Sarah Miller, Marta Guerrero Ble, and Bahati Kanyamanza. 2022. "2022 Global Refugee Work Rights Report." Center for Global Development, Asylum Access, and Refugees International.

Iqbal, Zaryab. 2007. "The Geo-Politics of Forced Migration in Africa, 1992–2001."
    Conflict Management and Peace Science 24 (2): 105–19.
Jarotschkin, Alexandra, Theresa Parrish Beltramo, Laura Abril Rios Rivera, Gonzalo Ignacio
    Nunez, Jedediah Rooney Fix, and Ibrahima Sarr. 2023. "Burundi Socioeconomic
    Survey: Results from the 2019–2020 Refugee Survey." World Bank, Washington, DC.
Kibreab, Gaim. 2007. "Why Governments Prefer Spatially Segregated Settlement Sites
    for Urban Refugees." *Refuge: Canada's Journal on Refugees* 24 (1): 27–35.
Nguyen, Nga Thi Viet, Aboudrahyme Savadogo, and Tomomi Tanaka. 2021. "Refugees in
    Chad: The Way Forward." World Bank, Washington, DC.
OECD (Organisation for Economic Co-operation and Development). 2023. "Development
    Finance for Refugee Situations: Volumes and Trends, 2020–21." OECD Publishing, Paris.
    https://www.oecd.org/content/dam/oecd/en/publications/reports/2023/11
    /development-finance-for-refugee-situations-volume-and-trends-2020-2021
    _46c7725d/cc2df199-en.pdf.
Pape, Utz Johann, Benjamin Petrini, and Syedah Aroob Iqbal. 2018. "Informing Durable
    Solutions by Micro-Data: A Skills Survey for Refugees in Ethiopia." World Bank,
    Washington, DC.
Sarzin, Zara, and Olive Nsababera. 2024. "Forced Displacement in Sub-Saharan Africa:
    A Stocktaking of Evidence." Background paper for the Africa Region Companion
    Report to *World Bank 2023: Migrants, Refugees, and Societies*, World Bank,
    Washington, DC.
UNHCR (United Nations High Commissioner for Refugees). 2023. "2023 Global Compact
    on Refugees Indicator Report." UNHCR, Geneva. https://www.unhcr.org/sites/default
    /files/2023-11/2023-gcr-indicator-report.pdf.
UNHCR (United Nations High Commissioner for Refugees). 2024. "Mid-Year Trends 2024."
    UNHCR, Geneva. https://data.unhcr.org/en/documents/details/111704.
UNHCR (United Nations High Commissioner for Refugees). 2025. "Sustainable
    Programming: What Is Sustainable Programming and Why Is It Needed?" UNHCR,
    Geneva. https://data.unhcr.org/en/documents/details/114423.
Vancluysen, Sarah. 2022. "Deconstructing Borders: Mobility Strategies of South Sudanese
    Refugees in Northern Uganda." *Global Networks* 22 (1): 20–35. https://doi.org/10.1111
    /glob.12322.
World Bank. 2019. "Informing the Refugee Policy Response in Uganda: Results from the
    Uganda Refugee and Host Communities 2018 Household Survey." World Bank,
    Washington, DC.
World Bank. 2023a. *World Development Report 2023: Migrants, Refugees, and Societies*.
    Washington, DC: World Bank.
World Bank. 2023b. "The Global Cost of Inclusive Refugee Education: 2023 Update."
    World Bank, Washington, DC.

PART II

Self-Reliance as a Foundation for a More Efficient and Humane Approach to Hosting Refugees

CHAPTER 2

Using Poverty Lines to Measure Refugee Self-Reliance

Why Measure Self-Reliance?

Self-reliance became a priority outcome of refugee support in recent years, with international discourse shifting from long-term care and maintenance models of assistance to promotion of refugee self-reliance. Key agreements such as the New York Declaration for Refugees and Migrants (2016), the Comprehensive Refugee Response Framework (2016), the United Nations Global Compact on Refugees (2018), and the call for sustainable responses (2024) all place emphasis on promoting refugee self-reliance, with many international organizations, nongovernmental organizations, and country governments now actively promoting self-reliance programs.

Despite this newfound consensus, a lack of understanding persists on what constitutes self-reliance and, by extension, how to measure it. Without an appropriate means of measuring refugee self-reliance, however, it is not only difficult to understand whether self-reliance has been achieved but also almost impossible to generate the systematic learning required for it to be achieved at scale.

To date, a handful of approaches have been used to measure refugee self-reliance, each with its own set of limitations. Most of these measures are at odds with the concept of self-reliance itself, allowing refugees who depend on humanitarian assistance to be identified as self-reliant. Moreover, these measures have been developed to reflect the refugee perspective, implicitly treating refugees' deprivations as distinct from those experienced by nationals, creating an artificial dichotomy that may curtail the consideration of joint host-refugee solutions.

This chapter introduces an alternative measure of self-reliance, one anchored in global poverty measurement and using a simple, one-dimensional indicator: consumption. Refugees are considered self-reliant if their consumption from nonhumanitarian sources exceeds the poverty line relevant to their context. To be self-reliant, it is not sufficient for refugees to have a standard of living above the poverty line; rather, they must reach the poverty line without relying on humanitarian aid. This approach necessitates that refugees generate sufficient income to pay for their consumption, giving self-reliance a welfare connotation and reflecting the requirement to be active in the labor market. Anchoring refugee self-reliance in poverty measurement not only legitimizes the measure but also is consistent with the notion that the yardstick used to assess nationals' welfare—and to measure poverty globally (Sustainable Development Goal Target 1.1)—is equally valid to measure refugees' welfare.

Review of the Literature on Measuring Self-Reliance

The most widely used definition of refugee self-reliance comes from the UN Refugee Agency, which defines self-reliance as

> the ability of an individual, household or community to meet essential needs and to enjoy social and economic rights in a sustainable manner and with dignity. By becoming self-reliant, refugees and displaced persons lead active and productive lives and are able to build strong social, economic and cultural ties with their host communities. Self-reliance can assist in ensuring that persons of concern are better protected by strengthening their capacity to claim their civil, cultural, economic, political and social rights. (UNHCR 2014, 7)

Self-reliance has emerged as a priority outcome of refugee support in recent years. However, the centrality of self-reliance to international refugee discourse marks more of a resurgence than an innovation, with self-reliance a repeated goal of assistance actors for over a century (Easton-Calabria 2022). Since its emergence in 1920s Greece, when the League of Nations provided livelihood assistance to over 1.5 million refugees, self-reliance has had many different incarnations, all of which have repackaged similar practices under different monikers, such as "self-sufficiency," "self-supporting," "rehabilitation," "self-help," "rural animation," and "Sustainable Responses" (Betts 2021; Easton-Calabria 2022; Easton-Calabria and Omata 2018; UNHCR 2025). Although refugee self-reliance has existed for over a century in its various forms, self-reliance has rarely been measured.

The most cited measures of refugee self-reliance are the Self-Reliance Index, "the first global tool to measure the progress of refugee families on their journey to self-reliance";[1] and the refugee self-reliance measure from Betts et al. (2018), which is used to assess how well-adapted refugee settlements are to supporting refugees. Despite representing the preeminent (if not only) recognized measures on refugee self-reliance, neither adequately accounts for independence from aid, thereby failing to capture the true notion of "self-reliance." For instance, although both measures account for food security, they do so by measuring food consumption only, with no consideration given to its source (for example, whether it comprises food aid) and whether household food security needs can be met in the absence of external assistance. Both measures capture information on independence from aid as individual dimensions, but this information does not inform the self-reliance scores of all other domains. As such, increases in the Self-Reliance Index's food domain score, which would logically be interpreted as an increase in self-reliance in food, could be entirely due to increases in food assistance. This limitation applies to other domains in these indexes, with self-reliance scores under housing, education, health care, and other dimensions increasing when outcomes improve, regardless of whether these improvements are due to assistance. In fact, independence from aid is so limited in the Self-Reliance Index that a household's self-reliance score can fall by a maximum of only 20 percent, even if the entirety of the household's needs are met by external assistance.

This chapter presents a more simplified measure of self-reliance based on consumption from nonhumanitarian sources. This indicator does not incorporate the range of dimensions found in other existing measures; however, by focusing on nonhumanitarian consumption, it arguably captures the most critical aspects of self-reliance: the ability to meet one's physiological and basic material needs independently of aid. In fact, given the challenging environments in which many refugees live, and the primacy attached to physiological and material needs in such situations, ensuring that these minimum, essential needs are met is of paramount importance. This focus would likely be diluted and overshadowed if less important and more extraneous factors were incorporated (Greeley 1994).

By anchoring self-reliance to a minimum level of consumption, self-reliance measurement follows the tradition of poverty measurement. Doing so brings two distinct advantages. First, it grounds the measurement of self-reliance in poverty measurement, thus ensuring use of the same welfare concept for refugees and nationals. Second, by linking self-reliance to the consumption aggregate, and not its constituent elements, the measure allows for substitution between different categories of consumption. For instance, an individual opting to spend large amounts on clothes while saving on food can still be self-reliant if his/her overall level of consumption exceeds the minimum threshold, even if so little money is spent on food that, based on caloric intake, the person might be considered food insecure.

A measure of self-reliance based solely on consumption may not be satisfactory to all (Appel 2025). For some readers, the proposed concept of refugee self-reliance may seem too narrow and lacking representation of specific challenges faced by refugees, such as restrictions on their right to work, their freedom of movement, or their access to health and education services. To some extent, however, the existing measurement already accounts for these factors. If labor market or mobility limitations are binding, refugees will not be able to earn much income and will fail to reach the level of consumption that would make them self-reliant. Similarly, if refugees have no access to education or health care, their income-generating capacity will be undermined, which will be reflected in the income they earn and their consumption. Viewed this way, the proposed self-reliance indicator captures not only a minimum acceptable standard of living but also, implicitly, how much discrimination and exclusion refugees experience.

This reasoning will not appeal to all. Moreover, just as global welfare measurement has expanded to report on multidimensional poverty (of which monetary poverty is an important component), one can consider a multidimensional self-reliance measure that captures both monetary self-reliance, as proposed in this chapter, along with indicators on access to services and infrastructure. Like the monetary self-reliance indicator, such a multidimensional self-reliance measure would be anchored in global poverty measurement if it bases itself on the World Bank's Multi dimensional Poverty Measure (Diaz-Bonilla 2022).

Using Poverty Lines to Measure Monetary Self-Reliance

The necessity to identify a minimum acceptable standard of essential needs is not unique to self-reliance. Welfare analytics of the most destitute in society faced a similar challenge in the 1990s, and resolved it by defining a "poverty line": those consuming less than the poverty line are poor, whereas those consuming more are nonpoor.

Poverty lines have been adopted globally and can be set in different ways. Typically, they are derived from nutritional requirements—a minimum caloric amount—and then complemented with the cost to satisfy nonfood essentials (clothing, shelter, private expenditure on education and health, and so on) obtained from households whose total (food) consumption equals the cost of obtaining the nutritional requirements. Poverty lines are typically calculated using data from consumption surveys and as such reflect the actual consumption and revealed preferences of households. Poverty lines are thus context-specific; that is, they reflect the consumption needs for achieving the minimum standard in a given society at a given time (Ravallion et al. 2008). By implication, each country sets its own national poverty line.

International comparisons typically do not rely on national poverty lines but use the international poverty line (IPL), itself derived from the national poverty lines of the world's poorest countries. The first IPL, based on research by Ravallion, Datt, and van de Walle (1991), was set at PPP$1.02[2] per day per person and became known as the dollar-a-day poverty line. Since then, the IPL has been updated with some regularity, with the latest produced in 2022 following the release of the 2017 PPPs. In that iteration, the IPL was defined as the median of the national poverty lines of 28 of the world's poorest countries and set at PPP$2.15, with Sustainable Development Goal 1 using it as a benchmark for poverty eradication (Jolliffe et al. 2022). With the 2017 PPP update came the recognition that the IPL may be too low to act as an acceptable minimum standard of living for middle-income countries, and subsequent global poverty lines for lower-middle-, upper-middle-, and even high-income countries were published thereafter.

In the remainder of this report, global poverty lines are used to explore self-reliance across Sub-Saharan Africa, with refugees deemed self-reliant when their consumption from nonhumanitarian sources exceeds the applicable global poverty line.

$$s_i = 1 \text{ if } y_i > z, else\ 0 \tag{2.1}$$

In equation (2.1), s_i is the self-reliance indicator of refugee i, z is the global poverty line, and y_i is nonhumanitarian consumption (that is, it deducts gifts, either in-kind or cash, received from humanitarian agencies from the consumption aggregate).

The self-reliance indicator can be expressed as the average incidence of self-reliance among the refugee population as follows:

$$S = \frac{1}{n}\sum_{i=1}^{q}\left(\frac{z-y_i}{z}\right)^0 \tag{2.2}$$

In equation (2.2), n is the number of refugees and q the number of refugees who are self-reliant. Note that, for refugees to be self-reliant, their nonhumanitarian consumption y_i has to exceed the poverty line z so that the bracketed term equals 1 for self-reliant refugees. This is, of course, a complex way of writing down the fraction of self-reliant people, but doing so has the advantage of clarifying how the self-reliance indicator S relates to the Foster-Greer-Thorbecke (*FGT*) family of poverty metrics (Foster, Greer, and Thorbecke 1984), defined as

$$FGT_\alpha = \frac{1}{n}\sum_{i=1}^{p}\left(\frac{z-y_i}{z}\right)^\alpha, \qquad (2.3)$$

where n is the number of people and p is the number of people who are poor nationals. When humanitarian assistance is zero, as it typically will be for nationals, then when α equals zero (poverty incidence) it holds that $FGT_0 + S = 1$: the fraction of poor nationals plus the fraction of self-reliant nationals equals 1, because a national is either poor or self-reliant. For refugees, this axiom does not hold because they are considered nonpoor if their total consumption exceeds the poverty line but are self-reliant only when their nonhumanitarian consumption exceeds the poverty line.

Refugees' Poverty and Self-Reliance in SSA

The measurement of refugees' consumption and poverty is an evolving field, and microdata sets that can be used for this purpose are increasingly available. This report uses microdata sets from five African host countries (Chad, Ethiopia, Kenya, Niger, and Uganda) with suitable data for estimating poverty and consumption among refugees and host communities (table 2.1).[3] Together these five countries host more than one-half of the refugees in Sub-Saharan Africa. In four of these countries (Chad, Ethiopia, Kenya, and Uganda), the data can be broken down into refugees living in camps and those living elsewhere, enriching the analysis.

Because the analysis involves comparisons across countries, it uses global poverty lines instead of national ones.[4] Poverty among refugees is found to be very high, ranging from 57 percent in Kenya to 75 percent in Ethiopia (figure 2.1). Poverty is also significant among host communities—those living within 15 kilometers of refugee settlements—often surpassing national poverty averages but generally remaining lower than refugees' poverty rates. Although poverty among refugees tends to be higher than among hosts, this is not always the case; as shown in annex 2A, refugees living in Kenya's refugee camps of Dadaab, Kakuma, and Kalobeyei have lower levels of poverty than their hosts on average. Such a result is rare; and, when refugees are better-off than their hosts, it is usually in areas of well-being, such as access to health care, clean water, or education.

Table 2.1   Microdata Sets Used

Country	Survey name	Poverty line used (PPP$)	Survey year
Chad	4th and 5th National Harmonized Survey on Households' Consumption and Informal Sector	2.15	2018
			2022
Ethiopia	Socioeconomic Survey of Refugees in Ethiopia	2.15	2023
Kenya	Kalobeyei Socioeconomic Survey		2019
	Kakuma Socioeconomic Survey	3.65	2021
	Kenya Integrated Household Budget Survey		2016
Niger	Enquête Harmonisée sur le Conditions de Vie des Ménages	2.15	2018
Uganda	Refugee and Host Communities Household Survey	2.15	2018

Source: Original table compiled for this report.

Note: This table uses 2018 data for Chad. More recent data are available covering 2022. These data are reflected in the vignette in chapter 4, which considers changes over time. PPP = purchasing power parity.

Figure 2.1   Poverty Incidence among Hosts and Refugees, Selected Countries

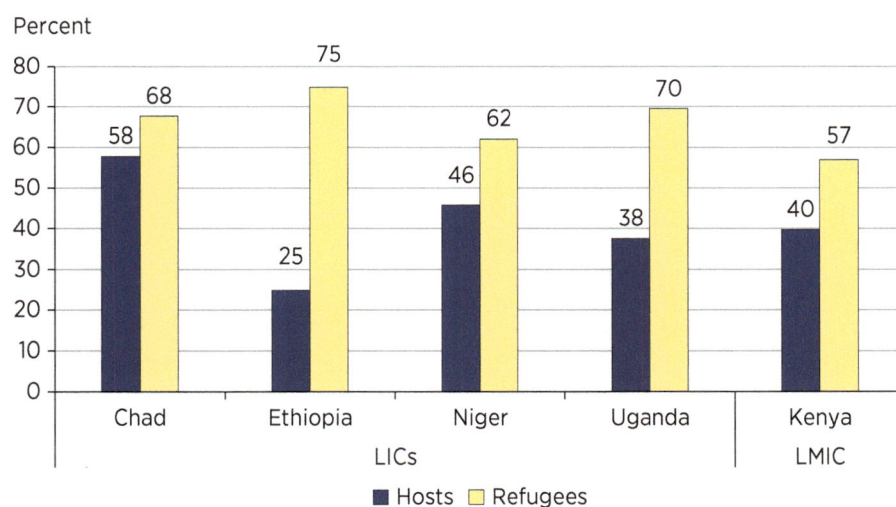

Source: Hoogeveen and Hopper 2024.

Note: Poverty lines used are provided in table 2.1. LIC = low-income country; LMIC = lower-middle-income country.

Aid received by refugees varies within and between countries, as shown in figure 2.2, which presents aid received by refugees in current US dollars.[5] The figure illustrates stark between-country differences in the degree to which refugees are assisted, with poor refugees in Ethiopia receiving on average $311 per year, similar to those in Kenya and Uganda but two to four times more than those in Chad in 2018 ($149) and Niger ($86). Within countries significant differences also arise in assistance: refugees residing in camps or settlements tend to receive the most assistance, whereas refugees living outside camps receive very little. For instance, poor refugees living in Kampala receive on average $27 per year, whereas those living in settlements receive 10 times as much. Even larger differences occur among refugees in camps and cities in Ethiopia and Kenya.

Aid significantly reduces poverty among refugees, as may be expected (refer to annex 2A). Its contribution to poverty reduction is largest in Kenya and Uganda, where refugees' poverty reduces by almost 25 percentage points due to the provision of aid.[6] By contrast, in Niger, where refugees receive little aid, the decline in poverty is just 7 percentage points. Figure 2.3 uses these data to show how much it costs, on average per refugee, to reduce poverty incidence by 1 percentage

Figure 2.2   Aid Received by Poor Refugees per Year, Selected Countries and Locations

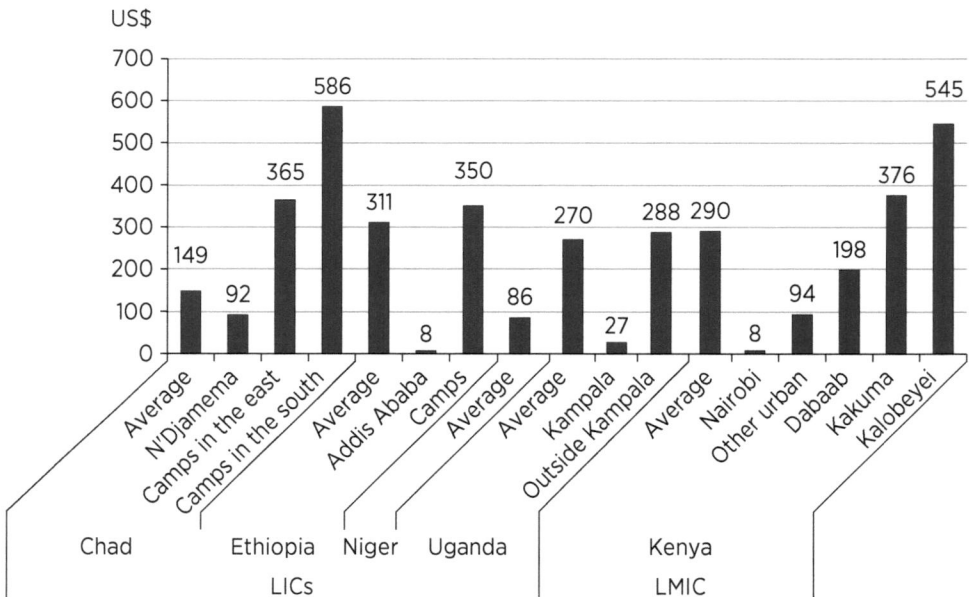

Source: Hoogeveen and Hopper 2024.

Note: Poverty lines used are provided in table 2.1. LIC = low-income country; LMIC = lower-middle-income country.

Figure 2.3   Cost of Reducing Refugees' Poverty by 1 Percentage Point, Selected Countries

US$

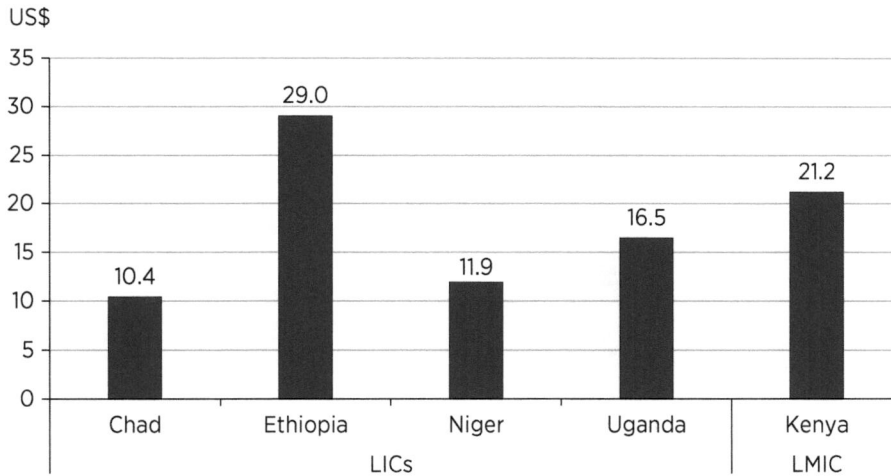

Source: Hoogeveen and Hopper 2024.

Note: Poverty lines used are provided in table 2.1. LIC = low-income country; LMIC = lower-middle-income country.

point in each country. These numbers should be interpreted with caution: even when aid does not reduce poverty it may be spent well to alleviate the suffering of the extreme poor but still be insufficient to take them across the poverty line. With this caveat in mind, figure 2.3 demonstrates the large variation that exists in the efficiency with which aid dollars can reduce refugees' poverty. In Chad and Niger, $10–$12 per refugee "buys" a 1-percentage-point reduction in refugees' poverty. In Ethiopia, three times more money is needed for poverty incidence to fall by 1 percentage point. Interpreted differently, if poverty reduction was the only objective of aid distribution to refugees, then a reallocation of aid resources between countries would achieve greater results.

Refugees are less self-reliant than their hosts, with hosts far more successful than refugees in attaining a minimum level of self-earned consumption in all the countries examined in this report (figure 2.4). This difference should not come as a surprise. Refugees have typically lost many or all of their physical assets, are traumatized by their experiences, face reduced human and social capital, and frequently experience significant restrictions with respect to labor market access and freedom of movement. Nonetheless, the fact that only 14 percent and 15 percent of refugees in Uganda and Ethiopia, respectively, earn incomes high enough to take their consumption over the poverty line is troubling, especially because 75 percent (Ethiopia) and 63 percent (Uganda) of hosts earn sufficient income to do so. These gaps highlight the severe economic hardship faced by refugees.

Figure 2.4   Self-Reliance among Hosts and Refugees, Selected Countries

Percent

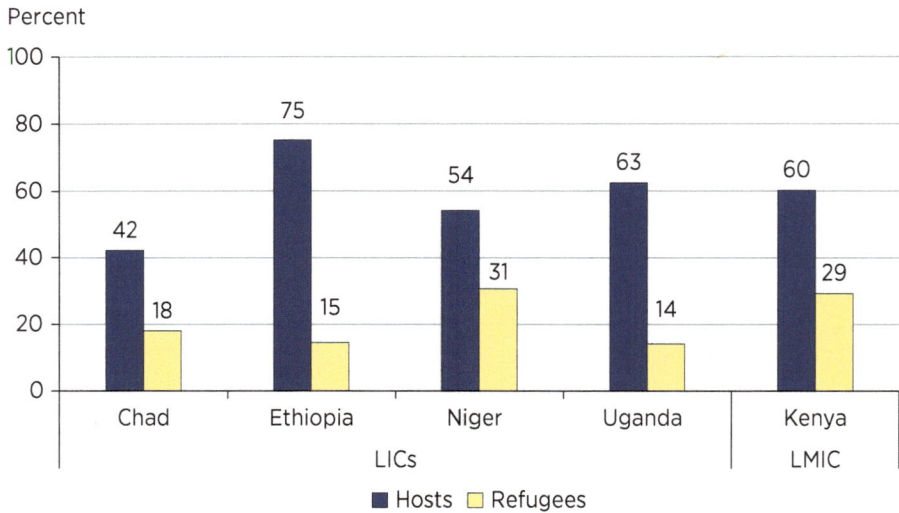

Source: Hoogeveen and Hopper 2024.

Note: Poverty lines used are provided in table 2.1. LIC = low-income country; LMIC = lower-middle-income country.

Low levels of self-reliance among refugees can be attributed to a loss of productive capacity caused by forced migration, the limited opportunities available to them in host countries, or a combination of the two. The considerable variation in self-reliance among refugees within the same country suggests that these challenges cannot be solely ascribed to a loss of productive capacity. Refugees residing in camps tend to have low levels of self-reliance (figure 2.5). By contrast, the degree of self-reliance among refugees in urban areas is much higher and almost on par with that of hosts, except in Ethiopia[7] (refer to annex 2A). In addition, between-camp variation is significant, with camps located in more remote areas with fewer economic opportunities (for example, Kakuma and Kalobeyei in Kenya) typically characterized by lower levels of self-reliance than those near population centers and trade routes (for example, Dadaab camp in Kenya).[8]

In combination, this information strongly suggests that a key driver of refugee self-reliance is the environment in which refugees operate. In places with ample economic opportunities, refugee self-reliance is high; where economic opportunities are limited, self-reliance is low. This finding does not imply that the productive capacity of refugees is intact. On the contrary, it is plausible that a process of self-selection takes place whereby the most capable

Figure 2.5   Refugee Self-Reliance, by Location, Selected Countries

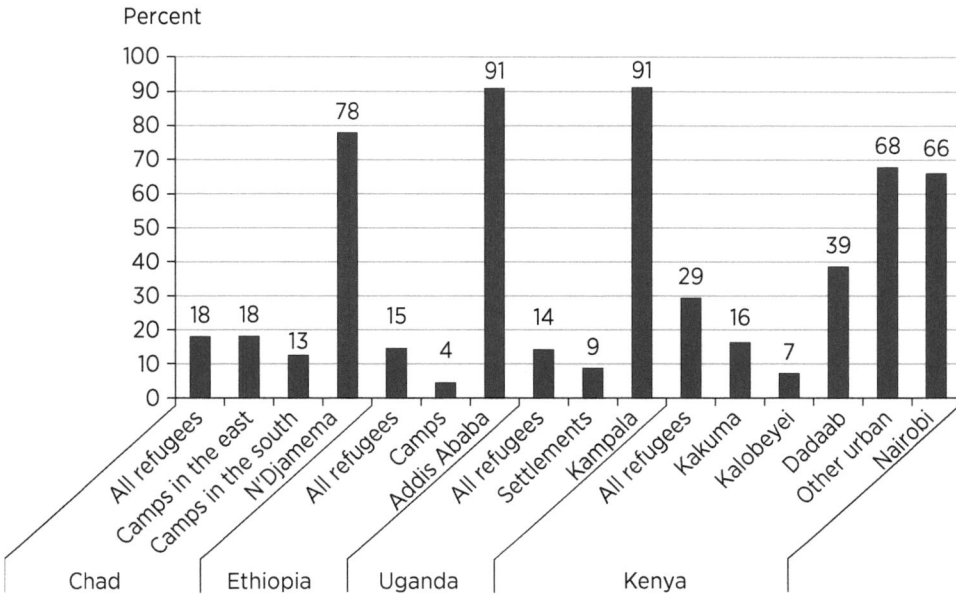

Source: Hoogeveen and Hopper 2024.

refugees—those with the greatest endowments of human and physical capital—end up in urban environments, and the most vulnerable refugees remain behind in camps. What it does imply, however, is that restoring the productive capacity of encamped refugees, without also improving the economic opportunities available to them, is unlikely to greatly improve self-reliance.[9]

Self-reliance is also negatively correlated with subsistence aid[10] at national and subnational levels. Consider figure 2.6, which shows that Niger, a country with very high levels of refugee self-reliance, receives the least assistance. One way to interpret this correlation is that subsistence aid provides a disincentive to work, an explanation made less plausible by the fact that the amount of aid is limited and the degree of destitution high among refugees. In such an environment, one would expect refugees, when given the opportunity to work, to take it.[11] What is more likely is that countries with severe restrictions on refugees' ability to work and earn a living create aid dependency, suggesting a relationship between a country's economic policies relative to refugees and the cost of international assistance.

Figure 2.6   Subsistence Aid Received by Poor Refugees as a Share of the Poverty Line, and Refugee Self-Reliance, Selected Countries

Percent

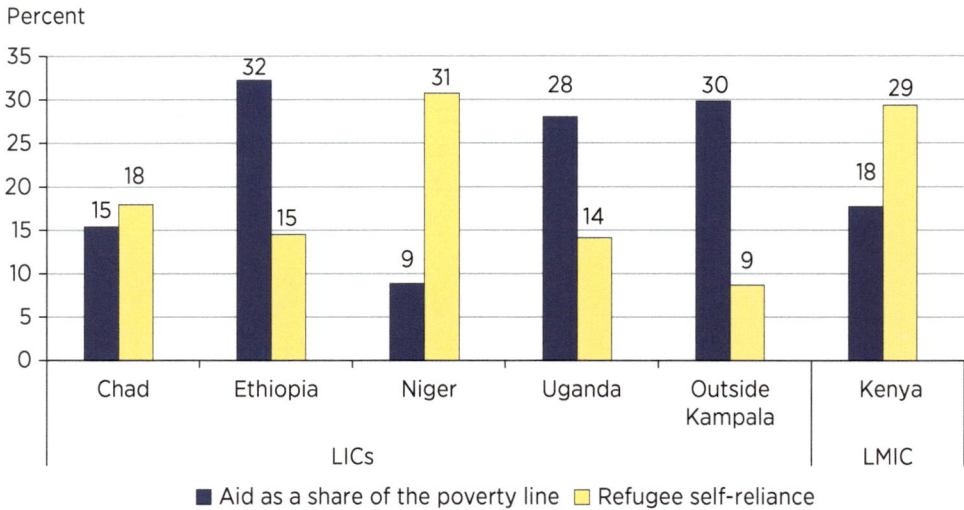

Legend:
■ Aid as a share of the poverty line   □ Refugee self-reliance

Source: Hoogeveen and Hopper 2024.

Note: Poverty lines used are provided in table 2.1. LIC = low-income country; LMIC = lower-middle-income country.

This pattern is evident both across and within countries: poor refugees receive less subsistence aid in areas that show higher self-reliance. In particular, urban refugees, who tend to be more self-reliant, receive significantly less assistance than those living in camps, even when they experience similar levels of poverty (figure 2.7). In Chad, for instance, poor refugees in N'Djamena receive 3 percent of the IPL in subsistence aid versus 15–19 percent received by refugees in camps. In Ethiopia, these differences are even larger, with poor refugees in camps receiving on average 36 percent of the IPL compared to just 1 percent for those living in Addis Ababa. Similar patterns are found in Kenya, with poor refugees in Nairobi also receiving 1 percent of the global poverty line on average, compared to refugees in Kalobeyei, who receive on average 33 percent. These gaps suggests that the default model of refugee assistance in camps—one that supplants refugees' socioeconomic rights with external assistance—likely increases dependence among its recipients and inhibits their self-reliance.

**Figure 2.7   Self-Reliance and Subsistence Aid Received by Poor Refugees as
Share of the Poverty Line for Refugees Living in Different
Locations**

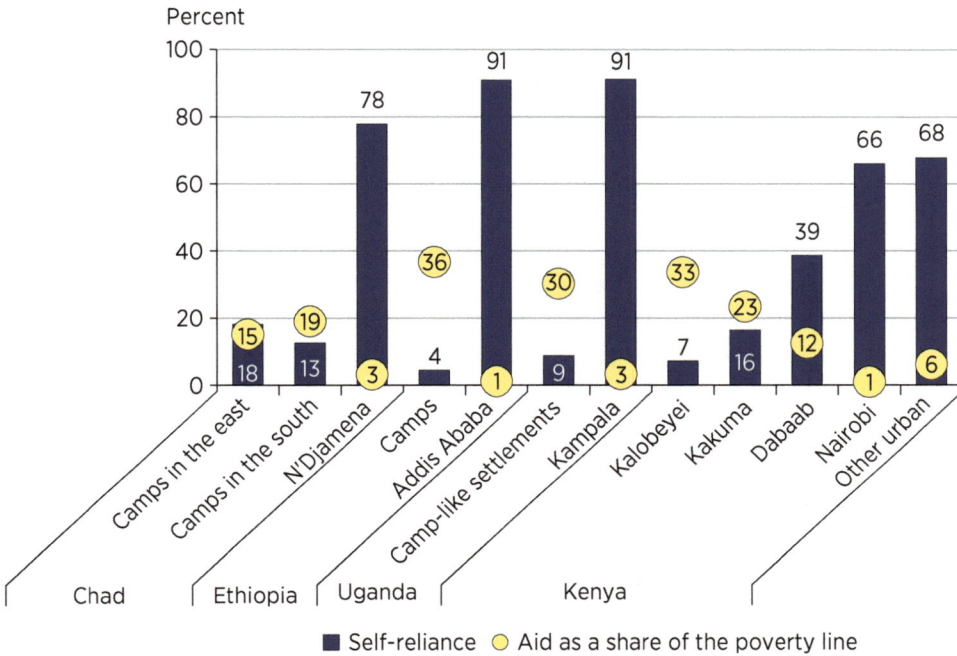

Source: Hoogeveen and Hopper 2024.

Note: Poverty lines used are provided in table 2.1. LIC = low-income country;
LMIC = lower-middle-income country.

Conclusion

This chapter presents a simple approach to measuring refugee self-reliance, one
that has several advantages over alternative available measures. It determines
refugee self-reliance through a quantifiable and widely understood metric:
consumption from nonhumanitarian sources. By avoiding a refugee-specific
indicator, the proposed measure anchors refugee self-reliance within existing
poverty measurement and the monitoring of Sustainable Development Goal
Target 1.1 (elimination of extreme poverty).

In its empirical section, this chapter shows that refugee self-reliance is low and typically below that of hosts, who themselves often have elevated levels of poverty and low levels of self-reliance. These findings help explain why refugees typically earn little income. They are frequently hosted in remote locations with limited economic opportunities and restricted access to external markets, hindering their self-reliance. Even host communities—which have not experienced the trauma of forced displacement, lost their productive assets, or faced restrictions on their right to work—are typically poor and lack self-reliance. Under such circumstances, it is no wonder that refugees typically remain dependent on aid and experience low levels of self-reliance.

This chapter also finds evidence that subsistence aid and self-reliance are inversely correlated. In settings in which refugees are less likely to be self-reliant, levels of aid are typically higher; in settings in which refugees are more self-reliant, levels of aid are often lower. Whereas this correlation makes sense from a humanitarian perspective—subsistence aid is given where it is most needed—from a development perspective it suggests a perverse incentive in that more aid is spent in environments where refugee self-reliance is hindered.

Because subsistence aid and refugees' incomes are substitutes, a better alignment of resources can be envisaged in which governments that encourage refugees to be self-reliant receive more aid. Such an approach would allow for the redirection of resources presently spent on humanitarian purposes to development purposes instead. This approach would benefit not only refugees, who would gain financial autonomy and self-reliance, but also hosts, who, as demonstrated in this chapter, often face high levels of poverty and at times are even poorer than refugees. Investments in the development potential of host regions and their communities will thus benefit refugees and hosts alike, increasing the incomes and self-reliance of all. Chapter 3 considers these aspects in greater detail.

Annex 2A. Summary Statistics on Poverty and Self-Reliance among Hosts and Refugees

Table 2A.1   Summary Statistics on Poverty and Self-Reliance among Hosts and Refugees, PPP$ 2.15

Country	Hosts			Refugees			
	Poverty incidence (%)	Self-reliance (%)	Poverty incidence (%)	Poverty incidence using nonhumanitarian consumption (%)	Poverty gap using nonhumanitarian consumption (%)	Aid[b] (%)	Self-reliance (%)
Chad	57.6	42.4	68.2	82.2	42.4	15.4	17.8
N'Djamena	—	—	17.5	22.1	9.5	2.8	77.9
Camps in the east[a]	—	—	66.1	81.9	37.8	14.7	14.7
Camps in the south[a]	—	—	79.3	87.5	60.7	18.5	18.5
Ethiopia	24.9	75.1	74.8	85.5	65.0	32.2	14.5
Addis Ababa	17.8	82.2	7.3	9.1	2.1	0.8	90.9
In camps[a]	31.7	68.3	83.7	95.6	73.3	36.3	4.4
Niger	45.8	54.2	62.1	69.3	32.2	8.9	30.7
Uganda	37.5	62.5	69.5	85.9	56.3	28.0	14.1
Kampala	3.1	96.9	2.7	8.8	2.9	2.8	91.2
Outside Kampala[a]	41.3	58.7	74.2	91.3	60.1	29.8	8.7

Source: Hoogeveen and Hopper 2024.

Note: PPP = purchasing power parity; — = not available.

a. Indicates a refugee camp or settlement.

b. Aid is expressed as a percent of the poverty line.

Table 2A.2 Summary Statistics on Poverty and Self-Reliance among Hosts and Refugees, PPP$ 3.65

Country	Hosts		Refugees				
	Poverty incidence (%)	Self-reliance (%)	Poverty incidence (%)	Poverty incidence using nonhumanitarian consumption (%)	Poverty gap using nonhumanitarian consumption (%)	Aid[b] (%)	Self-reliance (%)
Kenya	39.8	60.2	57.0	70.7	38.9	17.7	29.3
Kakuma[a]	87.1	12.9	69.9	83.7	49.5	22.9	16.3
Kalobeyei[a]	87.1	12.9	72.2	92.8	63.5	33.2	7.2
Dadaab[a]	61.0	39.0	44.5	61.4	27.9	12.1	38.6
Nairobi	22.5	77.5	33.1	33.9	9.8	0.5	66.1
Other urban	19.7	80.4	30.7	32.2	11.9	5.7	67.8

Source: Hoogeveen and Hopper 2024.

Note: PPP = purchasing power parity.

a. Indicates a refugee camp or settlement.

b. Aid is expressed as a percent of the poverty line.

Notes

1. Refugee Self-Reliance Initiative, "Self-Reliance Index (SRI)" (access May 24, 2024), https://www.refugeeselfreliance.org/sri.
2. PPP stands for purchasing power parity.
3. In deriving the consumption aggregate, special attention was paid to how humanitarian gifts are recorded. In certain surveys, it was in the consumption module itself; in others, it was collected through a special "assistance" module. Another area of attention was the value attached to shelter, a gift for many encamped refugees and as such deducted when calculating the (nonhumanitarian) consumption aggregate.
4. Unless otherwise indicated, poverty is measured by the international poverty line of PPP$ 2.15 for low-income countries, and by the global poverty line of PPP$ 3.65 for lower-middle-income countries.
5. All calculations convert 2017 PPP dollars into current US dollars using an exchange rate of 1.23 current US dollars for every PPP dollar (January 2024). The data presented capture aid delivered to poor households only, with aid received by nonpoor refugees (leakage) omitted from the analysis.
6. The contribution of aid to poverty reduction is calculated by subtracting poverty incidence based on nonhumanitarian consumption from poverty incidence using the full consumption aggregate.
7. Self-reliance is highest in Addis Ababa and Kampala and lower in Nairobi, where refugee (work) freedoms are relatively restricted. Kenya's legislation, for instance, prohibits refugees from working and requires them to live in camps (Betts 2021). Under such conditions, it is not surprising that refugees in Nairobi are less self-reliant than those in the comparatively freer city of Kampala. Nor is it surprising that refugees in Addis Ababa have such high levels of self-reliance: under its Out-of-Camp Policy, Ethiopia requires refugees to demonstrate that they can cover their cost of living and provide a sponsor before they are allowed to move out of camp (Kassa, Mulatu, and Edosa 2019).
8. Using a single poverty line to estimate refugee self-reliance can produce misleading results, particularly because the cost of living in urban areas is often significantly higher than in remote regions where camps or settlements are typically located. In Kenya, for example, the national urban poverty line is 82 percent higher than the rural poverty line. When applying these differentiated poverty lines, self-reliance among refugees living in remote Kakuma and Kalobeyei appears lower than that of refugees in Nairobi. In contrast, refugees in Dadaab demonstrate higher self-reliance levels than their counterparts in the capital.
9. This implication is supported by analyses for Ethiopia and Kenya, showing that, if refugees were given the opportunity to work in an urban area, they would increase their degree of self-reliance considerably, whereas, if they were given the opportunity to work in areas around the camps, their self-reliance would remain largely unchanged (Abeje, Cancho, and Hoogeveen 2025; Hoogeveen, Leander, and Nsababera 2024).
10. Subsistence aid received is calculated on the basis of all goods gifted to refugees, identified as such in the consumption module. Where appropriate, consumption value of shelter is also included in subsistence aid. Subsistence aid does not include benefits refugees receive from humanitarian services such as health or education.
11. Results from the Kenya Longitudinal Survey of Refugees and Host Communities (2021) support this expectation, because its data show that, of those employed, more than 75 percent would be willing to work more hours (if paid). Of the reasons given not to seek employment, a lack of available jobs is the largest response category (refer to the Kenya vignette in chapter 4).

References

Abeje, Fikirte, Cesar Cancho, and Johannes Hoogeveen. 2025. "The Case for Ethiopia's Refugee Jobs Compact Remains." Background paper for this report, World Bank, Washington, DC.

Appel, Tamar. 2025. "Measuring Refugee Self-Reliance. Developing a Definition and Framework for Measuring Self-Reliance of Refugees." Bachelor thesis, Wageningen University & Research.

Betts, Alexander. 2021. *The Wealth of Refugees: How Displaced People Can Build Economies.* Oxford University Press.

Betts, Alexander, Remco Geervliet, Claire MacPherson, Naohiko Omata, Cory Rodgers, and Olivier Sterck. 2018. "Self-Reliance in Kalobeyei? Socio-Economic Outcomes for Refugees in North-West Kenya." Refugee Studies Center, Oxford Department of International Development, University of Oxford.

Diaz-Bonilla, Carolina, Carlos Sabatino, Haoyu Wu, and Minh Cong Nguyen. 2022. "October 2022 Update to the Multidimensional Poverty Measure." Global Poverty Monitoring Technical Note, World Bank, Washington, DC.

Easton-Calabria, Evan. 2022. *Refugees, Self-Reliance, Development: A Critical History.* Bristol University Press.

Easton-Calabria, Evan, and Naohiko Omata. 2018. "Panacea for the Refugee Crisis? Rethinking the Promotion of 'Self-Reliance' for Refugees." *Third World Quarterly* 39 (8): 1458–74.

Foster, James, Joel Greer, and Erik Thorbecke. 1984. "A Class of Decomposable Poverty Measures." *Econometrica* 52 (3): 761–66.

Greeley, Martin. 1994. "Measurement of Poverty and Poverty of Measurement." *IDS Bulletin* 25.2, Institute of Development Studies.

Hoogeveen, Johannes, and Robert Hopper. 2024. "Using Poverty Lines to Measure Refugee Self-Reliance." Policy Research Working Paper 10910, World Bank, Washington, DC.

Hoogeveen, Johannes, Sebastian Leander, and Olive Nsababera. 2024. "Unpacking Spatial Variations in Refugee Self-Reliance in Kenya." Background paper for this report, World Bank, Washington, DC.

Jolliffe, Dean, Daniel Gerszon Mahler, Christoph Lakner, Aziz Atamanov, and Samuel Kofi Tetteh-Baah. 2022. "Assessing the Impact of the 2017 PPPs on the International Poverty Line and Global Poverty." Policy Research Working Paper 9941, World Bank, Washington, DC.

Kassa, Tadesse, Fasil Mulatu, and Jettu Edosa. 2019. "Ethiopia's Refugee Policy Overhaul: Implications on the Out of Camp Regime and Rights to Residence, Movement and Engagement in Gainful Employment." *Journal of Ethiopian Human Rights Law* 4 (1).

Ravallion, Martin, Gaurav Datt, and Dominique van de Walle, D. 1991. "Quantifying Absolute Poverty in the Developing World." *Review of Income and Wealth* 37 (4): 345–61.

Ravallion, M., and Franciso H. G. Ferreira. 2008. "Global Poverty and Inequality: A Review of the Evidence." Policy Research Working Paper 4623, World Bank, Washington, DC.

UNHCR (United Nations High Commissioner for Refugees). 2014. "A Global Strategy for Livelihoods: A UNHCR Strategy 2014–2018." UNHCR, Geneva. https://www.unhcr.org/sites/default/files/legacy-pdf/530f107b6.pdf.

UNHCR (United Nations High Commissioner for Refugees). 2025. "Sustainable Programming: What Is Sustainable Programming and Why Is It Needed?" UNHCR, Geneva. https://data.unhcr.org/en/documents/details/114423.

CHAPTER 3

Increased Refugee Self-Reliance and the Triple Win

Introduction

Refugees are often highly vulnerable and require significant support to meet their basic needs, particularly during the immediate aftermath of displacement; however, assistance should not render them passive recipients. Many refugees are able and eager to contribute through work in their host country. Participation in the labor market—as workers, farmers, or entrepreneurs— fosters financial independence, promotes self-reliance, and decreases reliance on external aid.

Support for meeting the subsistence needs of refugees is an important part of burden sharing. Broadly speaking, donors contribute to burden sharing by providing international assistance, whereas host countries contribute by providing refuge and allowing refugees to be economically active. This chapter presents data demonstrating that, although donors provide substantial financial resources for refugee assistance, these contributions are insufficient to fully meet refugees' subsistence needs. This finding should not come as a surprise given the analyses presented in chapter 2, which showed most refugees to be below the poverty line[1]. In contrast, host countries typically contribute to meeting refugees' needs through enabling their economic inclusion, albeit not to the extent needed for them to become fully self-reliant; very few low- and middle-income countries offer refugees their full set of socioeconomic rights. Consequently, despite monumental efforts from both donors and host countries, many refugees remain unable to meet their subsistence needs through a combination of assistance and self-earned income.

Chapter 2 observed that more humanitarian aid goes to refugees in situations with low self-reliance, creating the perverse incentive whereby more humanitarian aid goes to situations that constrain refugees and less to situations that encourage self-reliance. The challenge lies in transitioning to a scenario in which less humanitarian assistance is needed because refugees are more self-reliant, with development aid incentivizing self-reliance by facilitating refugees' economic inclusion. The questions then become the following: How much could be saved on humanitarian assistance if refugees become more self-reliant? And how much of these savings could be reallocated from humanitarian assistance to development aid if self-reliance increases?

This chapter presents a simple methodology, developed by the UN Refugee Agency and the World Bank (UNHCR and World Bank 2024b), to estimate the cost of refugees' subsistence needs in Sub-Saharan Africa (SSA). It shows that nearly 62 percent of this cost is met through refugees' earnings, and it calculates a shortfall in assistance of $1.52 billion required to bring refugees' consumption on par with that of host populations. The chapter then discusses how this shortfall can be met by either increasing refugees' economic inclusion or increasing aid, with the former shown to be relatively more realistic. The last section discusses how increased economic inclusion creates the scope for a triple win that benefits hosts, refugees, and donors.

Estimating the Cost of Meeting Refugees' Subsistence Needs

Just as poverty lines can be used to measure self-reliance, as was done in chapter 2, they can also benchmark the cost of refugees' subsistence needs. After all, poverty lines cover basic caloric requirements as well as spending on critical nonfood items, such as clothing, shelter, transportation, and expenses for health and education. If one uses international and global poverty lines, the cost for basic needs per refugee per day can be put at PPP$2.15, PPP$3.65, and PPP$6.85 for low-income countries (LICs), lower-middle-income countries (LMICs), and upper-middle-income countries (UMICs), respectively.[2] The total (benchmark) cost for subsistence needs per country is then determined by multiplying the number of refugees in a country by its relevant poverty line, before scaling from a daily to an annual cost.

Refugees' subsistence needs can be financed from, broadly speaking, two sources: income earned by refugees and assistance provided to them. More self-earned income implies a need for less humanitarian aid; conversely, when incomes are lower, the need for assistance rises (refer to box 3.1 on measuring self-earned income). The amount of humanitarian assistance required for a given refugee-hosting country can be found by subtracting the income earned by refugees from the relevant benchmark cost of subsistence needs (that is, the relevant poverty line), as illustrated in figure 3.1. It also indicates that, if refugees earn no income at all, the amount of humanitarian assistance required equals the benchmark cost of subsistence needs. Conversely, if refugees' earned income is equal to or above the poverty line, they are deemed self-reliant and the amount of humanitarian assistance needed is zero.

Box 3.1 Measuring Refugees' Self-Earned Income

When exploring refugee self-reliance empirically, the analysis in this report interchangeably references income- and consumption-based measures of self-reliance. The definition of *self-reliance* introduced in chapter 2 (nonhumanitarian consumption above the poverty line) uses a consumption-based measure to underscore its close association with monetary poverty (consumption below the poverty line). This chapter, in which complementarity between refugees' self-earned income and assistance stands central, uses an income-based measure of self-reliance (self-earned income above the poverty line). In practice, the measures can be used interchangeably.

Income is difficult to estimate precisely through any household survey (Carletto 2022; Deaton 1997), even more so when much of it is earned informally or through self-employment, for instance, in agriculture. Rather than employing an estimate of income that combines the incomes earned by different household members from multiple income sources, household income is proxied by nonhumanitarian consumption. Such an approach requires two simplifying assumptions: (1) on balance, refugee households generate no net savings; (2) nor do they finance consumption by accumulating additional debt. These are stringent conditions, yet this approach is, in almost all circumstances, more attractive than its alternative of assessing household income directly.

The implication of the equivalence of nonhumanitarian consumption and refugees' self-earned income is that refugees' ability to collect remittances is considered part of a household's income-generating capacity.

Figure 3.1   **Benchmark Cost for Refugees' Subsistence Needs and the Diminishing Need for Humanitarian Assistance with Increased Refugee Self-Reliance**

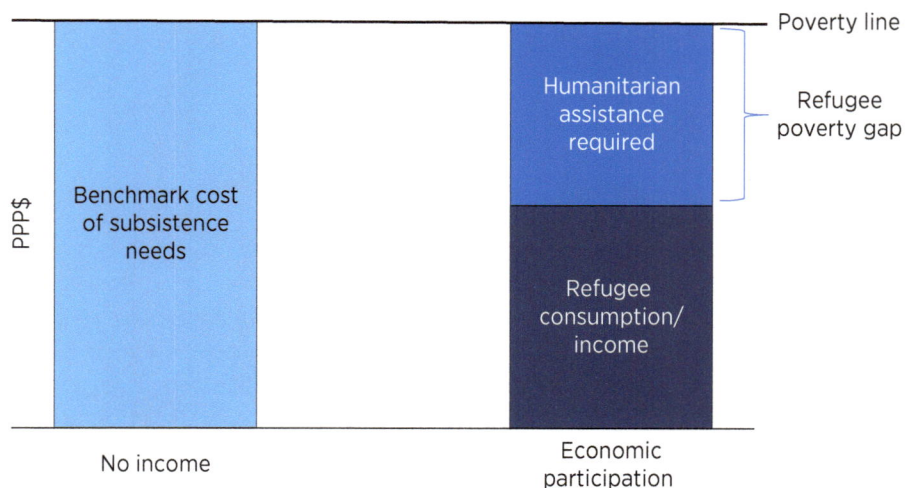

Source: Original figure created for this report.

Note: PPP = purchasing power parity.

The difference between the self-earned income of poor refugees and the poverty line—that is, the shortfall from the poverty line—is the so-called poverty gap (refer to Foster, Greer, and Thorbecke 1984). The amount of humanitarian assistance required to lift refugees above the poverty line can be found by multiplying the benchmark cost of subsistence needs with the poverty gap. If this humanitarian assistance is made available and perfectly targeted to refugees in need, then—through a combination of self-earned income and assistance— poverty among the refugee population would completely disappear. For hosts, however, poverty would likely remain.

As shown in chapter 2, host communities typically face elevated levels of poverty compared to the national population. Delivery of assistance to refugees that lifts them out of poverty would make refugees better-off than their hosts,[3] which would typically not be acceptable for many host governments. It is feasible, however, to adjust this benchmark so that the target for subsistence needs is equivalent to the host community's poverty gap, thereby ensuring that both groups are equally well-off. This report uses the host country poverty gap– adjusted benchmark for refugees not as an end goal in and of itself, but as a benchmark beyond which any assistance should be targeted in a nondiscriminatory way between refugees and hosts. Operationalizing this concept is straightforward: rather than humanitarian assistance being the difference between the poverty line and the self-earned income of poor refugees, assistance needs are measured as the difference between refugees' self-earned income and the host country poverty gap (figure 3.2).

Benchmark Cost of Subsistence Needs for Refugees in SSA

To estimate the benchmark cost of subsistence needs in SSA, poverty lines applicable to each country are used and multiplied by the number of refugees in each country. Because it compares costs across different countries, this report uses international, not national, poverty lines.

At mid-2024, approximately 9 million refugees resided in SSA, accounting for over one-fifth of all refugees globally. Of these refugees, 77 percent were in LICs, 21 percent in LMICs, and the remaining 2 percent in UMICs. The benchmark cost of subsistence needs for refugees in SSA—estimated by multiplying the number of refugees in each income category by the relevant poverty line—is estimated to be $10.4 billion, of which 65 percent is for refugees in LICs (figure 3.3), reflecting the high share of refugees hosted in countries like Chad, Ethiopia, Sudan, and Uganda.

Figure 3.2   Benchmark Amount of Humanitarian Assistance when Poor Refugees Are as Well-Off as Poor Hosts

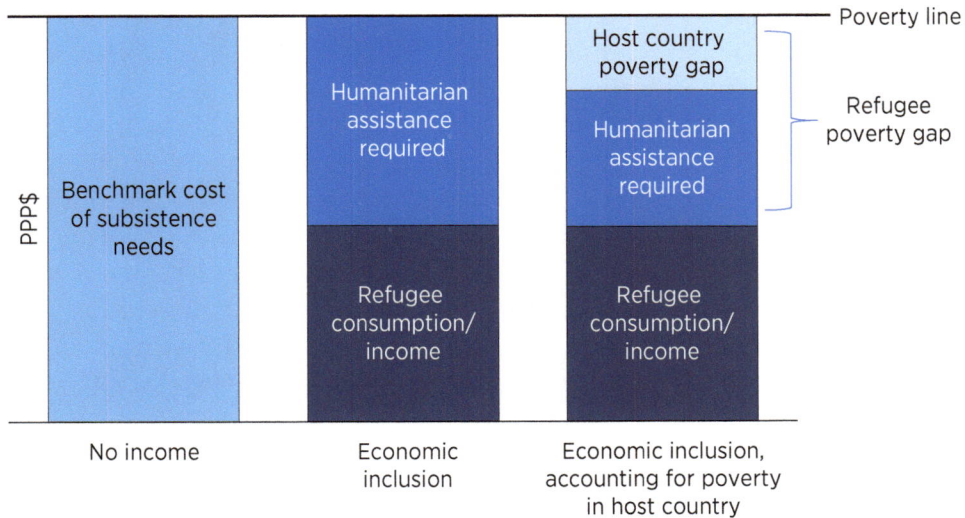

Source: Original figure created for this report.

Note: PPP = purchasing power parity.

Figure 3.3 Benchmark Cost of Subsistence Needs, by Country Income Category

US$, billion

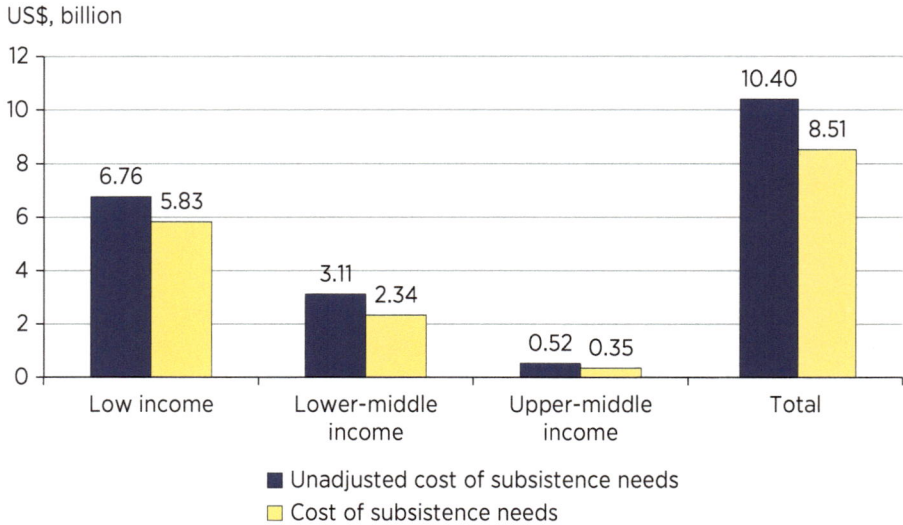

■ Unadjusted cost of subsistence needs
□ Cost of subsistence needs

Source: Original figure created for this report.

The resources required to meet refugees' subsistence needs inevitably reduce when hosts' average poverty gaps are used to benchmark refugee assistance. The World Bank regularly publishes its poverty gap index—measured using international and global poverty lines—on its Poverty and Inequality Platform; this information can be used to calculate the benchmark cost of refugees' subsistence needs so that refugees are, on average, as well-off as their hosts. For instance, if the poverty gap index for an LIC is 15 percent, or 0.15, its benchmark cost can be calculated using an adjusted poverty line of 0.85 * $2.15 = $1.83. Multiplying this *adjusted poverty line* by the number of refugees gives an adjusted benchmark cost of subsistence needs, with refugees no better- and no worse-off than hosts. Applying this calculation to all host countries in SSA, the total adjusted annual benchmark cost of subsistence for refugees falls by about 18 percent, from $10.40 billion to $8.51 billion. The remainder of this chapter uses this adjusted figure as the benchmark cost of subsistence needs, thus estimating the resources required to make refugees and hosts equally well-off.

Refugees' Self-Earned Income

To estimate refugees' self-earned incomes—and thus be able to calculate the additional resources required to meet the identified benchmark needs—refugee household survey data are required. The approach taken to identify self-earned income assumes that anything a refugee household consumes, and that is not provided by humanitarian agencies, has been obtained by the household itself through its own production, paid work, or remittances. That amount can thus serve as a proxy for self-earned income (refer to box 3.1). Relatively few data sets exist that make it possible to proxy refugees' self-earned income in this way, because they require the presence of an extensive consumption module and the identification of humanitarian assistance. For SSA, five such data sets exist for Chad, Ethiopia, Kenya, Niger, and Uganda. Chapter 2 used these same data sets to estimate monetary self-reliance. Fortunately, for the purposes of estimation, these five countries host about 57 percent of the refugee population in SSA.

To arrive at an estimate of income net of humanitarian assistance for all (poor) refugees in SSA, estimates of the refugee poverty gap derived from these five surveys are extrapolated.[4] Estimated refugee poverty gaps in Chad, Ethiopia, Kenya, Niger, and Uganda are 42 percent, 65 percent, 39 percent, 34 percent, and 56 percent, respectively. The refugee poverty gap was extrapolated using two approaches: (1) using poverty gaps weighted by the refugee population in each country (yielding an average poverty gap of 50 percent), and (2) using a simple geometric average of the poverty gaps (giving an average of 47 percent). Both approaches are equally defensible; and, in the absence of any additional information on refugee populations in different countries, an average poverty gap of 50 percent is assumed.[5]

Refugees' income is estimated using the complement of the refugee poverty gap. For the five countries for which data are available, actual figures are used; for the remaining countries in the region, 50 percent is used. This method finds that about 62 percent of the adjusted benchmark costs of subsistence needs (or $5.24 billion) are met through refugees' own earned income (figure 3.4), which underscores the important contribution of self-earned income and of host country policies in reducing the costs of hosting refugees.

Figure 3.4 Estimated Refugee Income, by Country Income Group

US$, billion

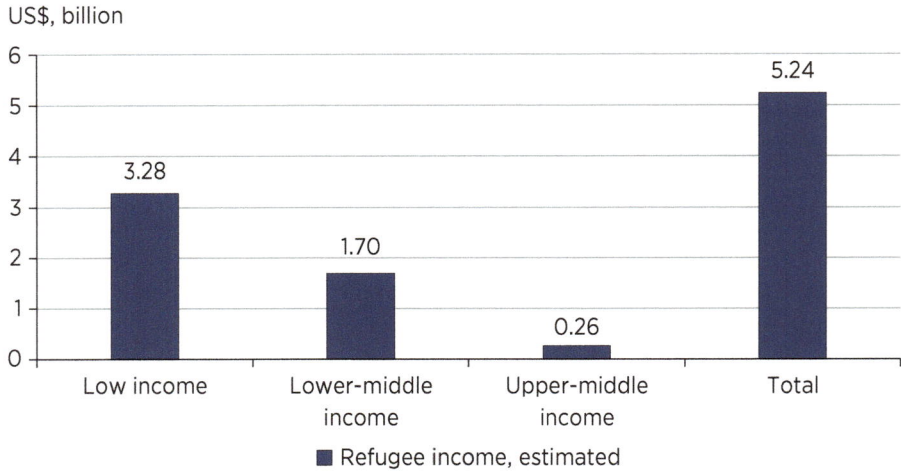

Legend: ■ Refugee income, estimated

Values shown: Low income 3.28; Lower-middle income 1.70; Upper-middle income 0.26; Total 5.24

Source: Original figure created for this report.

Humanitarian Assistance Needed and Provided

In the previous two sections, the benchmark cost of refugees' subsistence needs in SSA was estimated at $8.51 billion, using parity with host community consumption as the benchmark. The previous section also found that refugees earn an estimated $5.24 billion per year. If refugees could not work, the amount of assistance required for refugees to meet their subsistence needs would have been equivalent to the entirety of the benchmark cost. Because refugees do work, savings in humanitarian assistance are generated, with the total amount of assistance needed to bring refugees on par with hosts approximately $3.27 billion.

In practice, the amount of humanitarian assistance to meet the benchmark of subsistence for refugees will be higher because delivering aid comes with administrative costs as well as leakage to the nonpoor. International experience with large-scale social protection programs suggests that administrative costs are on the order of 2–8 percent, depending on the sophistication of the available administrative infrastructure (Grosh et al. 2022). Estimates of how much leakage one might have to account for are less clear. Hoogeveen and Obi (2024) estimate leakage from the assistance system in Jordan to be about 29 percent. It is not evident whether this degree of leakage would also be applicable to African countries, which tend to have higher levels of poverty and lower administrative capacity. In the absence of any other information, this section estimates that 137 percent (an additional 29 plus 8 percent) of $3.27 billion, or $4.48 billion, in humanitarian assistance would be required to make refugees as well-off as their hosts (figure 3.5).

To identify the shortfall in humanitarian assistance, the total amount of aid allocated to meeting refugees' subsistence needs in SSA is estimated. For the five countries for which microdata are available, figure 3.6 shows the following: the fraction of the poverty line that refugees cover with self-earned income, the fraction covered by humanitarian aid, and the shortfall in consumption relative to the poverty line. As before, the weighted average of aid received as a percentage of the poverty line is used to estimate the amount of assistance received annually by each refugee, which amounts to $193 per refugee. When multiplied by the number of refugees in SSA, the total amount of assistance directed toward refugees' subsistence needs in SSA is estimated at $1.75 billion.[6] These calculations find that humanitarian aid accounts for only about 54 percent of the total amount of assistance required to meet refugees' subsistence needs, with a shortfall in assistance of about $1.52 billion (excluding overhead).[7]

Figure 3.5   Annual Humanitarian Assistance to Make Refugees as Well-Off as Hosts, by Country Income Group

US$, billion

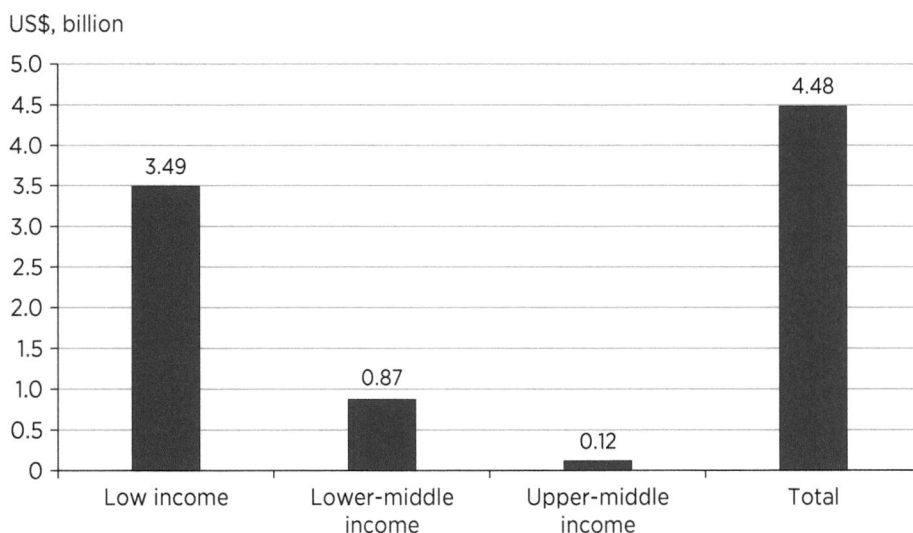

Source: Original figure created for this report.

Note: Calculations of the amount of assistance required account for overhead costs.

Figure 3.6   Sources of Consumption Financing Relative to the Poverty Line, Selected Countries

Percent of the poverty line

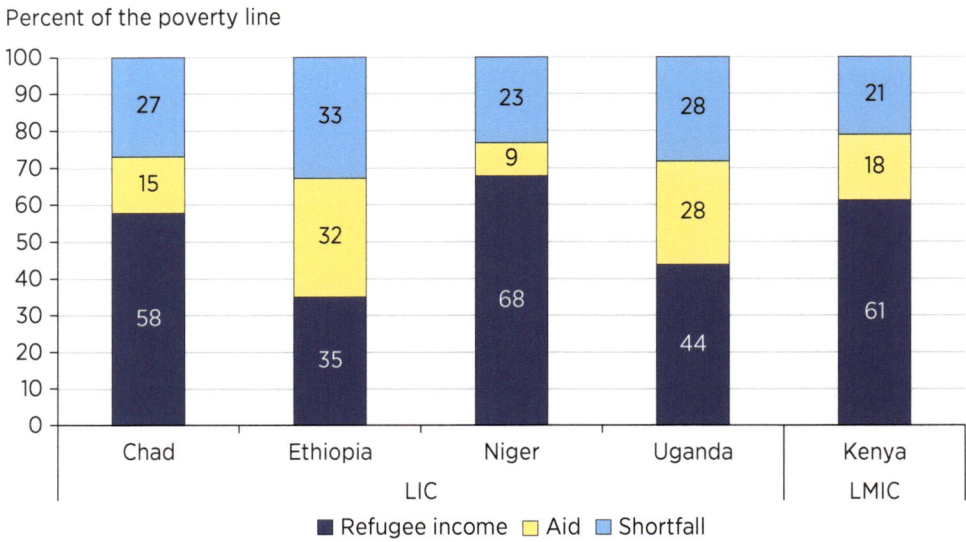

■ Refugee income   □ Aid   ■ Shortfall

Source: Original figure created for this report.

Note: LIC = low-income country; LMIC = lower-middle-income country.

Filling the Shortfall in Humanitarian Assistance

The previous section shows that $3.27 billion (excluding overhead) in assistance is required to bring all refugees in SSA to an acceptable standard of living—set here as a level of poverty comparable to that of their hosts. Of that required amount, just over one-half ($1.75 billion) is presently available as humanitarian assistance. Consequently, a significant shortfall persists in assistance, and refugees have significant levels of poverty, as already pointed out in chapter 2.

The common response to addressing this shortfall is that "more aid is needed." Figure 3.6 can be used to assess by how much aid would have to increase to bring refugees to the poverty line. In Chad and Kenya, aid would have to increase by 180 percent and 120 percent, respectively; in Ethiopia and Uganda, it would have to double; in Niger, an even greater increase of 250 percent would be needed. These numbers represent significant and challenging increases, and it is doubtful whether such increases in aid are realistic in the existing geopolitical context.

By contrast, if the shortfall were made up by increasing refugees' earnings, incomes would have to increase by 47 percent in Chad, 94 percent in Ethiopia,

34 percent in Niger and Kenya, and 64 percent in Uganda. Although also ambitious, these increases are achievable with the promotion of more sustainable approaches to refugee support, demonstrating clearly how strengthening refugee self-reliance may be the more effective and achievable avenue for meeting refugees' subsistence needs.

An interesting thought experiment is to explore what happens when poor refugees get the opportunity to earn, say, 25 percent more income. A 25 percent increase in the income of poor refugees raises it from $5.24 billion a year to $6.55 billion. This increase would reduce the amount required in assistance from $3.27 billion to $1.96 billion (excluding overhead), leaving a shortfall of just $0.21 billion if the total amount of humanitarian aid remains unchanged.[8]

A Triple Win

The previous section shows that strengthening refugee self-reliance reduces the amount required in humanitarian assistance. To illustrate this reduction more clearly, consider a hypothetical scenario with three parties: refugees, host countries, and international donors (with humanitarian agencies as implementing partners). Assume country X has a poverty line of $200 and hosts 20 refugees. Then the cost of meeting their subsistence needs is $4,000 when they are not economically active. Also assume that the host country allows refugees to work; 10 of those refugees are self-reliant, whereas the others earn no income. Then the cost of meeting the subsistence needs of poor refugees falls from $4,000 to $2,000. If financial donors provide humanitarian agencies with $1,000 to cover refugees' subsistence needs and the calculation abstracts from overhead, then each non-self-reliant refugee receives $100 and can meet only one-half of his/her subsistence needs.

This example highlights the current shortfall in burden sharing. Donors contribute $1,000 to burden sharing but fall short of the total amount needed to meet subsistence needs. Host countries facilitate economic inclusion but only to the extent that allows 10 refugees to be self-reliant. If the host country further eases access to employment and another three refugees find work that allows them to reach the poverty line (that is, they become self-reliant), then humanitarian agencies can reduce aid to non-self-reliant refugees and save $300.

What to do with these savings? One option is to leave the amount given to humanitarian agencies unchanged. If they continue to receive $1,000, they could spend more on the seven refugees who are not yet self-reliant. Alternatively, donors could reduce the amount of humanitarian aid to $700; in this case, nothing changes for non-self-reliant refugees, who continue to receive $100 each. It would, however, not be reasonable if this windfall benefits financial donors because it was the host country that increased its contribution to the global burden sharing by easing access to work. Why should financial donors capture the benefit of the increased effort by host countries? An alternative scenario is that the savings are distributed between the two parties concerned: refugees and host countries. Humanitarian agencies get to distribute an additional $150 among the seven poor refugees, and the host country receives $150 to be invested in economic development.

Although illustrative, this example demonstrates the existence of a triple win, in which refugees' welfare increases as they earn more income, increasing their financial autonomy, while more resources are channeled to the most vulnerable refugees. Host countries benefit because some of the humanitarian savings are channeled into development projects, and the international community gains because more money destined for development assistance is spent on investments in development projects and less on care and maintenance for refugees. The triple win can address the existing misalignment in which 66 percent of official development assistance funding for refugee hosting is for humanitarian purposes (OECD 2023), even though only some 22 percent of refugees are in emergency situations (OECD 2019), a mismatch that is particularly strong in SSA (figure 3.7).[9]

Figure 3.7 Distribution of ODA for Refugee Situations, Select SSA Host Countries, 2020–21

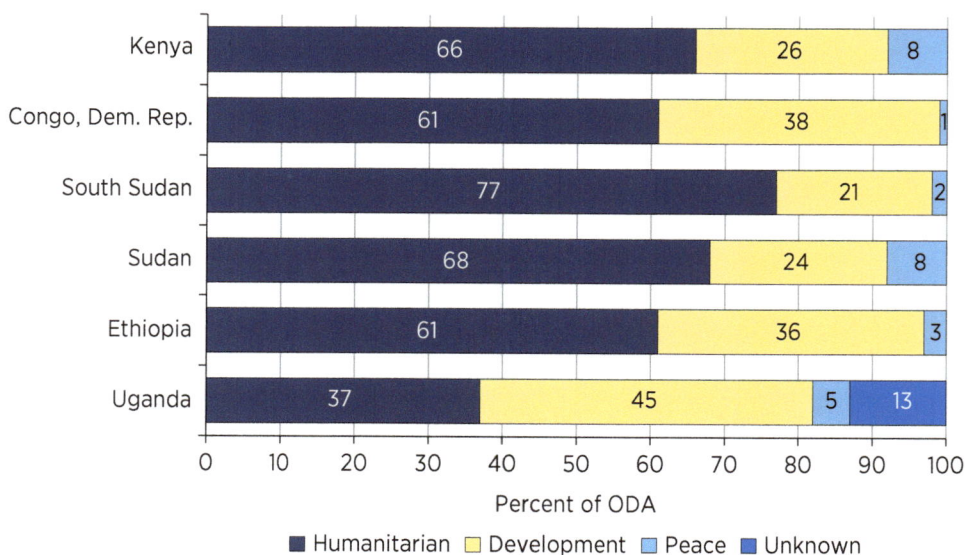

Source: Original calculations using OECD 2023.

Note: ODA = official development assistance.

Conclusion

The estimated benchmark cost of subsistence needs—or the cost of bringing the consumption of all refugees in SSA on par with hosts—is $8.51 billion per year. This report estimates that refugees already cover about 62 percent of the benchmark cost of subsistence needs through their own economic activity, equivalent to $5.24 billion per year.

The amount needed to bring refugees in SSA on par with hosts is thus $3.27 billion ($8.51 - $5.24 billion). Aid directed to subsistence needs is estimated at $1.75 billion, however, leaving a shortfall of $1.52 billion (excluding overhead and leakage) and creating a much higher level of poverty among refugees than among hosts. This situation indicates that, although donors contribute significant resources to burden sharing, these resources fall short, with aid having to almost double to bring refugees to an acceptable standard of living (parity with hosts). However, with financing to refugee situations tapering in recent years and with displacement expected to continue rising, a more promising strategy than relying on increased aid is to strengthen refugees' economic inclusion and self-reliance.

The thought experiment in this chapter estimates the savings associated with increasing poor refugees' earnings by a modest 25 percent. If this were to happen, refugees' earnings would increase from $5.24 billion to $6.55 billion, implying that the need for humanitarian assistance reduces by $1.31 billion. Assuming financial donors do not reduce their financial commitments to refugee-hosting countries and that this windfall was distributed equally between refugees and host countries, the financing of humanitarian donors would reduce by $655 million (about $900 million taking overhead into account);[10] at the same time, poverty among refugees would decrease, and the shortfall would drop from $1.52 billion to $865 million. Because the reduction in humanitarian aid is less than the increase in refugees' income, more assistance becomes available for the most vulnerable refugees. The other one-half of the windfall (the savings on humanitarian assistance, or $897 million or around $900 million) could be allocated to increased development assistance in refugee-hosting countries. If allocated through the World Bank, it would more than double the amount of resources available under the International Development Association's Window for Host Communities and Refugees.

Greater refugee self-reliance thus creates a triple win: (1) an increase in refugees' earnings and self-reliance, more aid for the most vulnerable refugees, and a subsequent fall in refugees' poverty; (2) reduced reliance on humanitarian assistance; and (3) additional development aid for host countries (figure 3.8). The latter can be used to address any negative distributional consequences that may be associated with refugees' inclusion and to stimulate economic activity and job opportunities to the benefit of both host populations and refugees.

This chapter shows that scope clearly exists for a mutually beneficial bargain between international donors and refugee-hosting countries. Under this bargain, international donors realize savings on humanitarian assistance thanks to enhanced refugee self-reliance and make part of these savings available for investments in jobs and economic development. Such investments have the potential to generate significant long-term benefits for their refugee and host recipients.

Figure 3.8   The Triple Win of Increased Refugee Self-Reliance

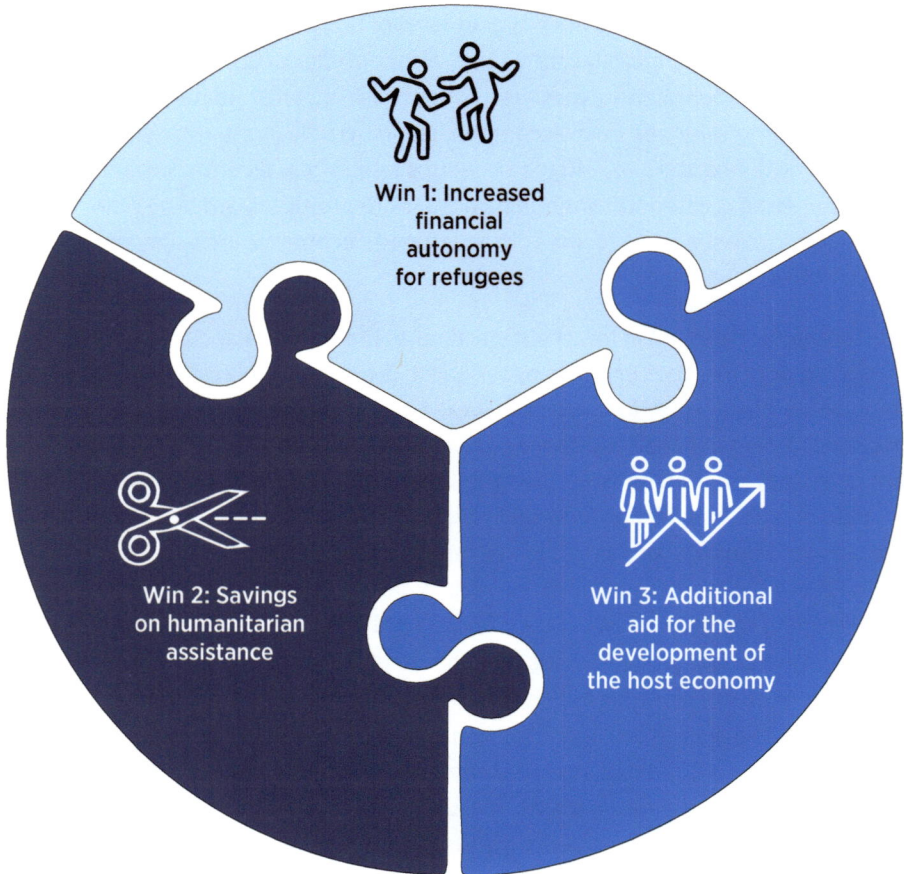

Source: Original figure created for this report.

Notes

1. Unless otherwise indicated, poverty is measured by the international poverty line of PPP$ 2.15 for low income countries, and by the global poverty line of PPP$ 3.65 for lower- middle-income countries. PPP= purchasing power parity.
2. PPP stands for purchasing power parity. To convert 2017 PPP dollars into current US dollars, an exchange rate of 1.23 current US dollars for every PPP dollar is used (January 2024). Each country's income classification is based on World Bank data as of the end of 2022.
3. In practice, the assumption of perfectly targeting assistance to refugees is not realistic. Even the most advanced social protection systems provide assistance to ineligible beneficiaries (mistargeting) or provide beneficiaries with more in assistance than necessary (waste). Because inefficiencies will occur when refugee transfer systems are implemented—and with these inefficiencies implying that some refugees end up in poverty because there will not be sufficient resources to bring all refugees to the poverty line—the notion that refugee poverty will be eliminated with the amount of humanitarian assistance calculated by the poverty gap alone is, strictly speaking, not correct.
4. The cost estimates in this report represent a best-effort projection based on the available data. Further efforts are essential to establish regular and systematic data collection on poverty among refugees and their host communities. Because they would enhance targeting, reduce inefficiencies, and potentially introduce beneficial conditionalities, such data are crucial for designing effective social assistance programs.
5. The extrapolation thus assumes that refugees across SSA have socioeconomic characteristics fairly comparable to those represented by the five countries. This assumption is broadly defensible (refer to, for instance, Figure 16 in Sarzin and Nsababera [2024] for a demographic profile of refugees across countries in the region).
6. To get $1.75 billion in the pockets of refugees, donor financing needs to be higher to account for administrative and leakage costs, as discussed earlier. The estimate is that it takes $2.39 billion in financing to have $1.75 billion reach poor refugees.
7. This shortfall represents a lower-limit estimate because a nontrivial share of humanitarian assistance is allocated to host communities.
8. Under the 20th replenishment of the International Development Association, $2.4 billion is available under the Window for Host Communities and Refugees, or about $800 million per year, because the International Development Association covers a three-year cycle.
9. Only in Uganda does development funding exceed humanitarian assistance for refugees, even though the fraction of humanitarian financing remains high.
10. $655 million is cash in hand for poor refugees. To deliver this support, overhead (estimated at 37 percent) has to be accounted for as well. If aid delivery can be reduced by $655 million, financial donors can reduce their funding to humanitarian agencies by $897 million.

References

Carletto, Gero, Marco Tiberti, and Alberto Zezza. 2022. "Measure for Measure: Comparing Survey Based Estimates of Income and Consumption for Rural Households." *World Bank Research Observer* 37(1): 1–38. https://doi.org/10.1093/wbro/lkab009
Deaton, Angus. 1997. *The Analysis of Household Surveys: A Microeconometric Approach to Development Policy*. Baltimore, MD: Johns Hopkins University Press.

Foster, James, Joel Greer, and Erik Thorbecke. 1984. "A Class of Decomposable Poverty Measures." *Econometrica* 52 (3): 761–66.

Grosh, Margaret, Phillippe Leite, Matthew Wai-Poi, and Emil Tesliuc, eds. 2022. *Revisiting Targeting in Social Assistance: A New Look at Old Dilemmas*. Washington, DC: World Bank.

Hoogeveen, Johannes, and Chinedu Obi, eds. 2024. *A Triple Win: Fiscal and Welfare Benefits of Economic Participation by Syrian Refugees in Jordan*. Washington, DC: World Bank.

OECD (Organisation for Economic Co-operation and Development). 2019. "Financing for Refugee Situations." OECD Development Policy Papers No. 24, OECD Publishing, Paris.

OECD (Organisation for Economic Co-operation and Development). 2023. "Development Finance for Refugee Situations: Volumes and Trends, 2020–21." OECD Publishing, Paris. https://www.oecd.org/content/dam/oecd/en/publications/reports/2023/11/development-finance-for-refugee-situations-volume-and-trends-2020-2021_46c7725d/cc2df199-en.pdf.

Sarzin, Zara, and Olive Nsababera. 2024. "Forced Displacement in Sub-Saharan Africa: A Stocktaking of Evidence." Background paper for the Africa Region Companion Report to *World Bank 2023: Migrants, Refugees, and Societies*, World Bank, Washington, DC.

UNHCR (United Nations High Commission for Refugees) and World Bank. 2024b. "Economic Participation and the Global Cost of International Assistance in Support of Refugee Subsistence Needs." World Bank, Washington, DC.

PART III

Making Refugee Self-Reliance Happen

CHAPTER 4

Country Vignettes on Self-Reliance

Introduction

This chapter explores the concept of self-reliance and the challenges surrounding its realization. A widespread and deeply engrained culture of both welcoming strangers and self-sufficiency exists in much of Sub-Saharan Africa (SSA). This culture is also reflected in legal conventions and policies, yet in practice it does not always translate into successful self-reliance outcomes. SSA has the largest fraction of refugees living in camps and camp-like settings, which is not conducive to self-reliance. Even in countries where refugees are granted freedom of movement and unrestricted access to labor markets, such as Niger and Uganda, refugees still end up clustered together in settings with limited economic opportunities.

This chapter presents four case studies that explore the elusive nature of refugee self-reliance in more detail. Based on background papers prepared for this report, these case studies provide a heuristic review of self-reliance in SSA, highlighting common challenges around fostering self-reliance.

Uganda: Self-Reliance through Access to Land

As of April 2025, Uganda had the largest refugee population in SSA, hosting approximately 1.9 million refugees. Approximately 92 percent of refugees live in more than 80 village-style settlements across the country, with the remaining 8 percent residing among host populations, predominantly in Kampala. Uganda's refugee settlements vary considerably in size, from about 2,500 refugees among the smaller settlements in Oruchinga and Rwamwanja districts to up to 70,000 refugees in Nakivale settlement in Isingiro District, with the median settlement hosting about 11,000 refugees.

For decades, Uganda's progressive refugee policies have resulted in positive gains for its refugees and host communities alike. The country's refugee response is integrated into its National Development Plan, and the country's vision is that refugees contribute to the development of host areas under its Comprehensive Refugee Response Framework. The legal and policy framework for refugees reflects a vision also outlined under the Global Compact on Refugees, permitting refugees significant freedoms. Established in the 2006 Refugees Act and 2010 Refugees Regulations, Uganda's refugee-hosting regulatory framework embodies five key refugee protection elements: (1) property rights and access to land; (2) the right to access employment and engage in income-generating activities; (3) the right to access public social services, including education and health; (4) freedom of movement and association; and (5) the right to documentation and equality before the law.

Uganda's model has three core components that distinguish it from many other host countries. First, refugees are allowed to work and choose their place of residence; second, refugees are allocated plots of land to cultivate in integrated rural settlements; and third, refugee-host interaction is encouraged. As such, unlike in most refugee camps, refugees living in Uganda's integrated settlements have the freedom to come and go at will, access markets outside of their settlements for trade and income-generating activities, and use local social service providers, all of which contribute to refugees' integration and self-reliance. Implicit in Uganda's integrated settlements model is the belief that most refugees will achieve self-reliance through agriculture on designated plots of land, which helps them become self-sufficient by growing their own food, generating an income, and thereby reducing their reliance on humanitarian aid.

Promoting the self-reliance of refugees through establishing sustainable livelihoods that will progressively reduce the need for humanitarian aid is thus a central component of Uganda's refugee model. In addition, efforts to strengthen local institutional capacity and enhance local service delivery in host areas are considered essential to minimizing disparities in access to basic services between refugees and hosts, and avoiding the inevitable tensions that would follow.

Uganda has long been recognized for its inclusive approach to hosting refugees and its readiness to promote self-reliance by offering access to land and jobs. At the same time, chapter 2 reported that refugees in Uganda exhibit the lowest degree of self-reliance among the five SSA countries examined, which represent the universe of data available on refugee self-reliance in the region. This vignette examines not only how access to land promotes self-reliance among refugees but also the challenges associated with Uganda's approach, which have led to such low levels of self-reliance among its refugee population.[1]

Correlates of Self-Reliance in Uganda

Although refugees in Uganda report feeling welcome and secure, the World Bank (2019) highlights the precarious conditions under which refugees in the country live. Almost 70 percent of refugees live in poverty, and 7 out of 10 refugee households experience food insecurity. The level of self-reliance among refugees is strikingly low, at just 14 percent (figure 4.1).[2] However, self-reliance is also limited among the host population, with just 49 percent earning sufficient income to be classified as self-reliant.

It is important to assess how the degree of self-reliance changes depending on the circumstances of refugees, such as employment status, access to land and land size, level of social integration, informal barriers to employment, and so forth. Descriptive analyses show that self-reliance among refugees with access to land of 0.05 hectare (ha) per capita or more is 30 percent, more than twice the average rate of self-reliance for refugees and five times larger than those with less than 0.05 ha per capita. Other factors that improve the degree of self-reliance among refugees are whether the head of household is working

Figure 4.1   Self-Reliance, by Refugee/Host Status and by Refugee Characteristics, Uganda

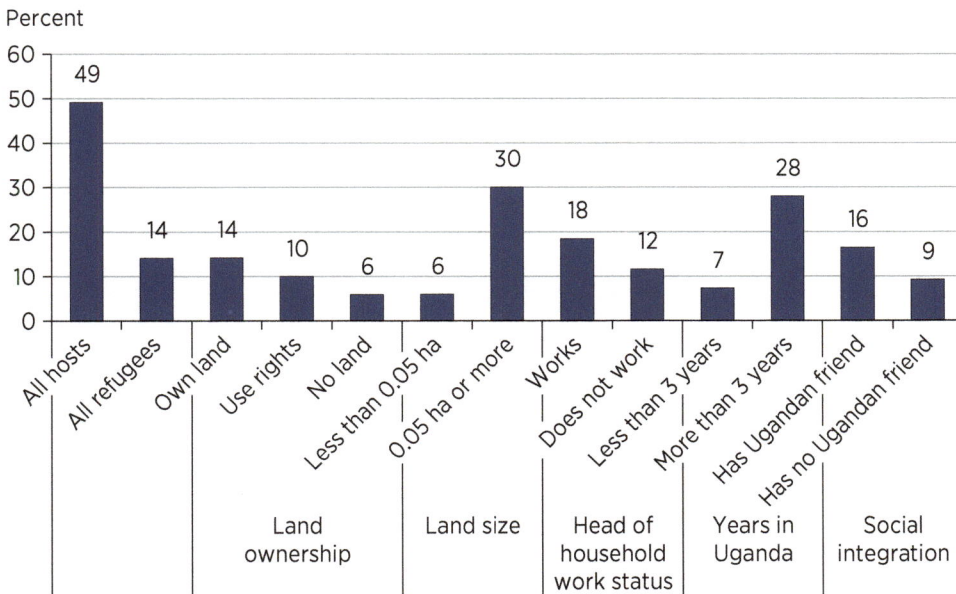

Source: Atamanov, Hoogeveen, and Reese 2024.

Note: ha = hectare.

(18 percent) or whether refugees with children have Ugandan friends
(16 percent). Duration of stay is positively associated with self-reliance too.
Refugees who have been in Uganda for three or more years are four times more
likely to be self-reliant than those who arrived more recently. These descriptive
results suggest that better economic and social integration of refugees, along
with access to productive assets such as land, is associated with increased
self-reliance.

To evaluate these correlations more formally, a simple regression model is used,
with the left-hand side variable the logarithm of the ratio of refugees'
nonhumanitarian consumption to the international poverty line (table 4.1).
A positive value for the dependent variable means refugees are self-reliant,
whereas a negative value means a lack of self-reliance (nonhumanitarian
consumption is lower than the poverty line). The household characteristics
discussed previously enter the regression as explanatory right-hand side
variables, along with variables measuring the number of mature cattle refugee
households own and whether households borrowed money or goods, or are
paying back money because of doing so. The dependency ratio is included as
well to proxy a household's capacity for work. These variables are expected to
affect refugees' ability to earn income and become self-reliant. Finally, the
regression controls for the region of residence, household size, age, sex, and
literacy of the household head. Variables with a positive sign are associated with
greater self-reliance, whereas variables with a negative sign are associated with
reduced self-reliance and with a widening of the gap between nonhumanitarian
consumption and the poverty line.

**Table 4.1   OLS Regression Results Explaining the Difference in the Log
Ratio of Refugees' Nonhumanitarian Consumption to the IPL,
by Refugee Household Characteristics, Uganda**

Variable	Coefficient
Head of household working (base = not working)	0.265***
Household owns at least one plot of land	
Household does not have land or have use rights on land	−0.168*
Household does not have land	
Household owns less than 0.05 hectare per capita	−0.116
Household owns at least 0.05 hectare per capita	0.263**

(continued)

Table 4.1   OLS Regression Results Explaining the Difference in the Log Ratio of Refugees' Nonhumanitarian Consumption to the IPL, by Refugee Household Characteristics, Uganda *(continued)*

Variable	Coefficient
Household has lived in Uganda one year or less	
Household has lived in Uganda 2 years	−0.0762
Household has lived in Uganda longer than 3 years	0.410***
Household child/children have Ugandan friend(s)	0.233***
One household member	
Two household members	−0.533**
Three household members	−0.537**
Four or more household members	−0.760***
Dependency ratio (children and elderly over total household size)	−0.712***
Head of household is literate	0.05
Number of cattle owned	0.0195***
Any member borrowed money or goods, or is paying back	0.289***
West Nile	
Kampala	1.806***
Southwest	0.259***
Head of household age	−0.00533*
Male head of household	−0.00418
Constant	−0.129
Observations	691
R-squared	0.578

Sources: Atamanov, Hoogeveen, and Reese 2024; Uganda Refugee and Host Communities Household Survey, 2018; original calculations.

Note: Regression is run for the refugee sample only using population weight. Positive coefficients mean greater self-reliance. IPL = international poverty line; OLS = ordinary least squares.

*** Significant at 1 percent, ** at 5 percent, * at 10 percent.

Consistent with the earlier descriptive analysis, several household characteristics are significantly correlated with greater self-reliance. Most notably, having an employed household head and having at least 0.05 ha of land per household member is significantly associated with improved self-reliance, as is social integration ("children have a Ugandan friend"). Given that integration takes time, staying in Uganda three or more years is understandably associated with improved refugee self-reliance compared to staying in Uganda only one to two years. Ownership of cattle and the ability to borrow are also found to be positively associated with self-reliance. The gender of the household head is not associated with self-reliance, after controlling for other characteristics of refugees and their location. Households with larger numbers of children or with more elderly persons tend to be less self-reliant, presumably because they have a lower capacity to work.

A simple comparison between refugees and Ugandan households demonstrates that refugees lag behind their hosts with regard to precisely those characteristics found to be associated with increased self-reliance (figure 4.2). For example, refugees are less likely to have access to land and, when they do, generally do not own it and instead have user rights only. The size of land also differs substantially between Ugandan and refugee households. Most Ugandans (76 percent) have at least 0.05 ha per capita, whereas most refugees have no land at all or less than

Figure 4.2 Differences in Selected Characteristics across Host and Refugee Households, Uganda

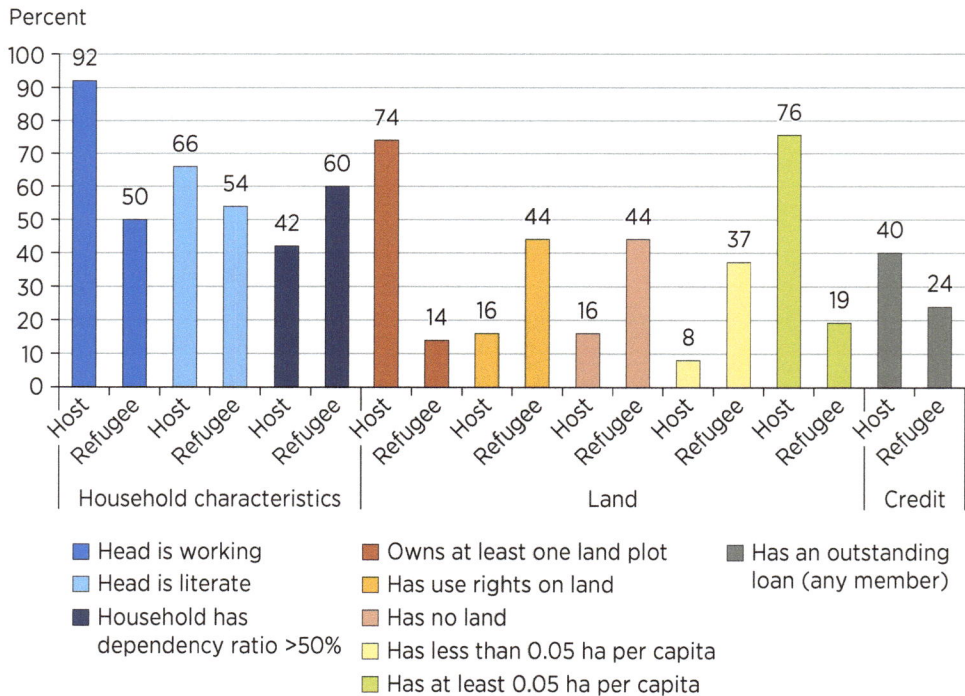

Source: Atamanov, Hoogeveen, and Reese 2024.

Note: ha = hectare.

0.05 ha per capita. Refugee heads of household are less likely to work and less likely to be literate compared to their Ugandan counterparts. Refugees have higher shares of children and elderly (dependents) compared to Ugandans, with dependents comprising 50 percent or more of refugee households, compared to 42 percent of Ugandan households. These characteristics show that refugees face significant constraints to self-reliance, many of which can be improved or overcome with intervention.

Reflection: Importance of Dispersion and Portable Assistance

The government of Uganda has created a legal environment that makes it possible to improve refugee self-reliance and reduce refugees' dependence on humanitarian assistance. The legal status accorded to refugees, most notably the right to participate economically, has brought them significant benefits. Betts (2021), for instance, reports how relative to refugees in Kenya, who are not afforded the same rights, refugees in Uganda are more mobile and face lower transaction costs because they tend not to be harassed by the authorities when traveling. Nevertheless, the evidence shows that refugees in Uganda exhibit low levels of self-reliance in both absolute and relative terms.

Two challenges are associated with Uganda's approach: (1) sites often identified for settlements are not suitable for agriculture; and (2) as more refugees arrive and existing settlements grow, the land available per refugee household declines. Betts (2021) and Bohnet and Schmitz-Pranghe (2019) describe in detail how the size and availability of plots decreased with the inflow of new arrivals. Initially, refugees were given a shelter plot measuring 15 meters (m) by 20 m as well as a cultivation plot measuring 50 m by 50 m. Over time, increasing demand led to decreasing agricultural plot size for both existing refugees and new arrivals, with plot sizes reducing to 20 m by 50 m or even 13 m by 20 m. In addition, soil fertility declined over time because of constant cultivation. Thus, as agricultural plots became smaller, they also became less productive.

This finding raises an important point. When too many people reside in the same location, access to land inevitably becomes a constraint. A simple calculation can illustrate. Assuming a farmer can walk for up to 30 minutes to reach his/her plot, fields must be within a 2-kilometer (km) radius of the village. Consequently, about 12.6 km^2 of cultivable land are potentially available. With an average population density in rural areas ranging from 100 people per km^2 in Moyo district in the far north to 440 people per km^2 in Kisora in the southeast, a settlement can host between 1,260 and 5,500 people depending on its location. Few refugee settlements in Uganda are this small, with most far larger,[3] indicating that a largely land-based self-reliance strategy is not viable in most host environments.

This is not to suggest that land-based refugee strategies cannot work. In fact, the results suggest the contrary. Refugees who can access sufficient land are more likely to be self-reliant. Rather, the implication is that, for a land-based strategy to work, refugees need to be more widely dispersed—that is, through either more and smaller settlements or the inclusion of refugees in existing villages. With 60,800 villages in the country, the average village would need to welcome fewer than 30 refugees, or approximately seven refugee families (assuming all refugees want to live in rural villages and do not go to urban areas).

A second observation, reported in chapter 2, is that refugees residing in Kampala, Uganda's capital city, are much more likely to be self-reliant (92 percent) compared to those in rural areas (only 9 percent). Refugees who opt to move to town are likely to have a greater appetite for risk, to be more entrepreneurial, and to have skills and connections that make them more likely to succeed. One finds that refugees in Kampala are more likely to be of working age (between 15 and 64 years old) and to have lower dependency ratios (World Bank 2019); for these reasons, the high levels of self-reliance among these refugees do not carry over to all others. Nevertheless, including refugees in urban areas, and making urban economic opportunities accessible to refugees, presents itself as a viable pathway to increasing refugee self-reliance.

It does not make much sense to expect a refugee who used to live in an urban area and who has never cultivated land before to be effective at farming, yet a considerable share of refugees originate from urban areas (figure 4.3). According to the Refugee Economies data set, 47 percent of refugees hosted in Nakivale lived in urban areas in their country of origin.[4] This situation highlights the importance of rural and urban solutions for the achievement of sustainable refugee solutions.

Given that many refugees in Uganda originate from urban areas, and that better opportunities arise for self-reliance in urban areas, one may ask why more refugees do not move from settlements to urban areas. After all, refugees have freedom of movement in Uganda. One explanation is that urban refugees are not eligible for general food assistance. Some manage to obtain it nonetheless by remaining registered in settlements; however, on average, poor refugees in urban areas receive much less assistance than those in settlements ($27 versus $288; refer to chapter 2). The near absence of assistance in urban areas may trap destitute refugees in settlements because they lack the financial means to move to areas with greater opportunities and cannot afford to risk moving in case they do not immediately find gainful employment. Moving to urban areas may also risk the loss of social networks developed in areas where refugees are first settled. These networks can be an important source of employment or insurance, suggesting that it may be more difficult to disperse refugees who have been in the host country longer than those newly arrived.

Figure 4.3   Location of Origin for Refugees, Selected Countries in East Africa

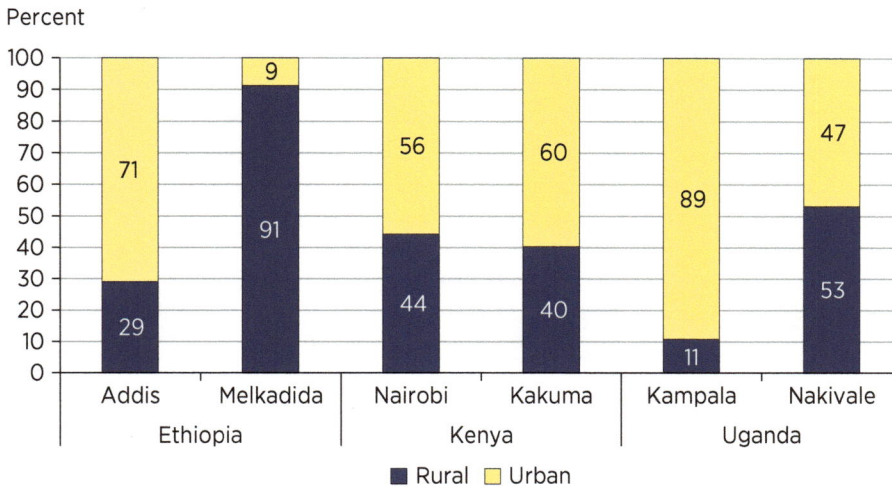

Source: Original calculations using the Refugee Economies, "Refugee Economies Programme: Dataset," https://www.refugee-economies.org/dataset.

Another explanation is that refugees may not want to leave behind the home and land they have for risk of losing it. They may prefer instead to designate select household members to move to town, while maintaining a foothold in the settlement. It seems plausible that, if humanitarian assistance were made portable, more refugees would try to move to areas where they would have greater chances of economic success, improving their self-reliance and reducing the need for humanitarian assistance in the long run.

Finally, domestic authorities may not want to promote a move to town. They are often nervous about the prospects of mass urban flows of refugees without sufficient economic opportunities because of the potential risks these flows pose to social services and social cohesion in urban centers. Thus, any transition to increase support for urban refugee-based solutions should be carefully sequenced and managed for unintended consequences facing host communities.

Niger: Making Progressive Refugee Policies Work Even Better

Niger is located at the heart of the Central Sahel region, an area beset by conflict and violence. Since 2012, vast numbers of refugees and asylum seekers have settled in Niger's southern and eastern regions, driven by coup d'états and insurgencies in Burkina Faso and Mali, as well as violence and instability in northern Nigeria, where "bandit" militia groups and conflicts with Al Qaeda, Boko Haram, and the Islamic State forced large numbers to flee to Niger (Center for Preventive Action 2024; UNHCR 2024a). Consequently, the number of refugees and asylum seekers in Niger rose significantly in recent years, reaching an estimated 431,072 people by April 2025.[5] Refugees from Nigeria make up the greatest proportion of the country's refugee population (61 percent), followed by those from Mali (29 percent) and Burkina Faso (10 percent), with the remaining 10 percent coming from Chad, Sudan, and other neighboring countries.

In addition to being the largest refugee-hosting country in West Africa, Niger has a significant population of internally displaced persons (IDPs), which since 2015 has dwarfed the country's refugee and asylum-seeking population. As of April 2025, Niger had more than 507,438 IDPs as well as an additional 47,274 "other people of concern," the latter largely comprising returnees from Niger escaping conflicts and insecurities in their adopted host countries (UNHCR 2024a).

Like Uganda but less well-known, Niger operates an inclusive set of policies regarding refugees. It offers refuge to those in need of international protection through an "out-of-camp" policy that not only aims to avoid settling refugees in permanent camps but also intends to promote local integration and self-sufficiency among all forcibly displaced persons (FDPs).[6] Most refugees in Niger live in informal sites or within host communities in rural and peri-urban areas. A small, urban refugee population resides in the cities of Agadez and Niamey, whereas the country's only refugee camp, Sayam Forage, is home to over 30,000 refugees, mainly from Nigeria, who are based in the camp for security reasons and free to move as they please (UNHCR 2023a).

Under the country's 1997 Refugee Law and implementing decree, refugees and asylum seekers are granted the right to work, freedom of movement, and access to national public services, as well as access to land, housing, and property rights—all on an equal footing with nationals. In addition, because almost all refugees are citizens of the Economic Community of West African States, they enjoy the same de jure rights as Nigeriens in the labor market under several treaties of that community. Refugees thus face little or no legal issues accessing employment in Niger, which is one of only four countries in SSA to offer refugees and asylum seekers full access to labor markets and national social security programs (UNHCR 2023a, 2023b).

Niger's inclusive approach to hosting refugees pays off: the country hosts the largest fraction of self-reliant refugees (31 percent) in SSA, more than twice as high as the proportion in Uganda. Furthermore, Niger has the smallest gap in self-reliance between refugees and hosts, indicating greater parity between refugees and hosts than in the four other SSA countries examined in this report. Despite Niger's exemplary refugee regime, however, 62 percent of refugees are poor compared to 46 percent of hosts, and self-reliance is lower among refugees, with 54 percent of hosts versus 31 percent of refugees self-reliant, suggesting that more is needed to improve refugees' welfare.

This vignette aims to uncover why refugees are so much worse-off than the host community. It explores three explanations: (1) having fled their place of origin, refugees have fewer endowments than their hosts; (2) refugees receive lower returns to their endowments because of discrimination; or (3) returns are lower for refugees simply because they are recent arrivals, forced to settle in the least attractive locations or use land of lower quality, and lack the experience and knowledge of local circumstances to fully exploit economic opportunities. To explore these possibilities, Niger's role as a host country for both refugees and IDPs is exploited. Conducting and comparing analyses on both refugee and IDP populations allows for a better understanding of the disparities between refugees and hosts.

Descriptive Statistics of FDPs in Niger

The demographic composition of Niger's two main refugee populations (Malian and Nigerian refugees) and of the country's IDP and host populations are broadly comparable, with similarities in the age of household head, household size, and household dependency ratio (table 4.2).[7] Human capital is also comparably low across all four population groups, albeit slightly higher among the host population, with refugees and IDPs showing similar education outcomes.

Table 4.2   Household Characteristics of IDPs, Refugees, and Hosts, Niger

Household characteristics	IDPs	Refugees, Malian	Refugees, Nigerian	Hosts
Personal characteristics				
Age of head	42	44	42	45
Head is female (%)	30	40	27	23
Household size	4.9	5.1	4.4	5.0
Share of dependents (%)	55	57	51	53
Education				
Average years of schooling	0.5	0.4	0.2	1.1
Share of head with no education (%)	92	94	96	82

(continued)

Table 4.2   Household Characteristics of IDPs, Refugees, and Hosts, Niger *(continued)*

Household characteristics	IDPs	Refugees, Malian	Refugees, Nigerian	Hosts
Share of head with primary education (%)	5	4	4	12
Share of head with secondary education (%)	3	2	1	5
Land and livestock				
Average land size, if work in agriculture (ha)	1.2	0.9	1.1	1.4
Land ownership, if work in agriculture (%)	17	0	2	77
Land ownership, all households (%)	27	1	14	38
Poultry (average number per household)	6.6	7.1	5.5	7.2
Ruminants (average number per household)	5.3	3.9	4.2	7.4
Employment				
Head works in agriculture (%)	41	20	18	44
Head works in industry (%)	36	64	51	36
Head works in services (%)	23	16	31	20
Head is self-employed (%)	85	53	77	82
Welfare				
Poverty incidence, at PPP$2.15/day (%)	62	92	52	46
Self-reliance (%)	28	5	28	54

Source: Coulibaly et al. 2025.

Note: ha = hectare; PPP = purchasing power parity.

Access to agricultural land and assets is higher among the host population, which is far more likely than FDPs to own land, farm larger plot sizes, and have poultry and ruminant livestock. Most notably, refugees have vastly inferior agricultural access and assets compared to hosts. Only 2 percent of refugees working in agriculture own land, compared to 77 percent of the host population. Additionally, refugees' plot sizes are 30 percent smaller than those of hosts on average, and refugees' ownership of ruminant livestock is nearly one-half that of the host population.

Primary income sources also differ significantly between population groups. The main source of employment for both hosts and IDP populations is agriculture, followed by industry and services.[8] For refugees, the picture is noticeably different: the main source of employment for both Malian and

Nigerian refugees is the industrial sector (55 percent of refugees who work),[9] with refugees also far less likely to be self-employed than hosts and IDPs, especially Malian refugees.

Table 4.2 shows that levels of poverty and self-reliance are worse for refugees and IDPs than for hosts. These differences are noticeably pronounced for Malian refugees, whose poverty and self-reliance outcomes fall far behind those of the host community. By contrast, welfare outcomes for Nigerian refugees and IDPs are remarkably similar.

Refugees in Niger are far less likely to be engaged in agriculture, have inferior access to agricultural land, and, consequently, demonstrate higher levels of poverty than hosts (table 4.2). Limited access to land for farming is costly for refugees. Regression analyses in a background paper for this report find that self-employment in agriculture is more likely than any other activity to increase earned income among refugees in Niger (Coulibaly et al. 2025).

Large differences in productivity per hectare exist among population groups, with refugees from Nigeria and hosts attaining comparable level but refugees from Mali demonstrating productivity levels just 5 percent of that attained by Nigerian refugees and hosts (table 4.3). A possible explanation for these differences is that refugees from Mali have largely settled in Niger's arid pastoral and agropastoral zones in the west near the Mali-Niger border, whereas refugees from Nigeria and a large fraction of IDPs have settled in the rainfed millet and sorghum belt in the country's southwest (UNHCR 2024a).[10] This differential pattern of settlement is also reflected in the use of organic fertilizers and pesticides, and the number of days worked on the land, which are far greater for Nigerian refugees and hosts than for Malian refugees and IDPs.

Table 4.3   **Agricultural Inputs and Outputs for Refugee, IDP, and Host Households Engaged in Self-Employed Agriculture, Niger**

Population group	Land size (ha)	Number of crops	Time to plot (minutes)	Days of labor	Use of organic fertilizer (%)	Use of pesticide (%)	Agricultural productivity (CFAF/ha)
Refugees, Nigerian	1.1	1.2	48	87	1.3	24.6	348,119
Refugees, Malian	0.9	1.7	52	47	0.0	0.0	20,250
IDPs	1.2	1.2	48	82	0.5	13.6	94,584
Hosts	1.4	1.2	44	98	2.3	19.0	371,888

Source: Coulibaly et al. 2025.

Note: CFAF = CFA franc; ha = hectare; IDP = internally displaced person.

Understanding the Causes of Lower Income among Refugees and IDPs

As the previous descriptive analysis suggests, although FDPs fare worse than hosts, differences arise in the experience of FDP groups. Most notably, Nigerian refugees and IDPs have comparable levels of self-reliance, whereas refugees from Mali fall behind. To understand the reasons behind these differential outcomes, Coulibaly et al. (2025) use Oaxaca-Blinder decompositions to explore how much of the differences in refugee, IDP, and host incomes[11] is due to observable characteristics (differences in endowments), and how much is due to unexplained factors (differences in returns), which in turn could be attributable to discrimination against foreigners (in the case of refugees), to location (if lower returns are associated with being a refugee from Mali and settling in the west of the country), or to other, as-yet unobserved characteristics.

Figure 4.4 shows outputs from five separate Oaxaca-Blinder decompositions. It shows how the differences in (log) income between FDPs and hosts are overwhelmingly due to unexplained factors—that is, differences in returns. Specifically, only 28 percent (0.14/0.48) of the differences in income between refugees and hosts is the result of differences in observed characteristics, which can be eliminated by restoring refugees' endowments to levels comparable to those of hosts. This means that 72 percent (0.34/0.48) of the difference in income between refugees and hosts is due to either differential returns on endowments or factors omitted from the model. Comparing hosts with Malian refugees and Nigerian refugees separately yields similar results, which suggests that, although refugees lose numerous productive assets (physical, financial, human, and social) when fleeing their homes, much of the observed differences in income between refugees and hosts result from unexplained factors and lower rates of return. For IDPs, the distinction is smaller, with only 48 percent (0.13/0.28) of the difference in income between IDPs and hosts unexplained by the model. Although less, this difference still reveals that almost one-half of the differences in income between hosts and IDPs results from lower rates of return on IDP endowments, rather than from differences in their endowments.

Most differences in income between refugees and hosts are thus due to lower rates of return on refugees' endowments, rather than to differences in endowments between these groups. These differential returns may be the consequence of several factors, including poor economic environment, discrimination, or a latecomer effect. The latter refers to the disadvantages faced by FDPs as a result of being new arrivals to host areas, which may result in their accessing lower-quality, marginal lands and having inferior economic relations with the host population. In many remote, rural locations where small, informal economies preside, the economy is often embedded in social and cultural relations, rather than operating as an isolated area. Because economic activity

Figure 4.4   Oaxaca-Blinder Decomposition of Log Income between Hosts and FDP Groups, Niger

Difference in log income

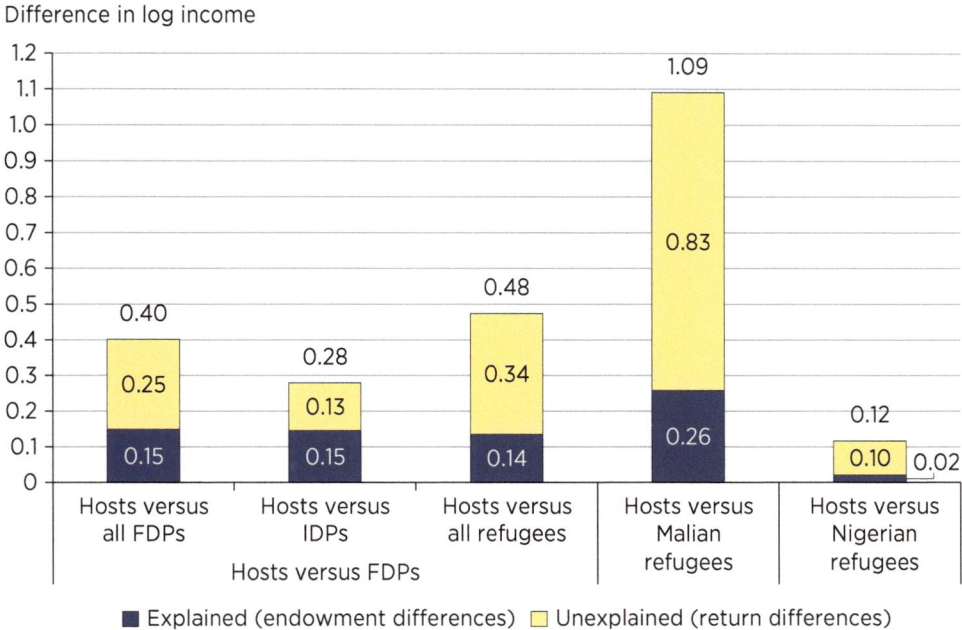

Source: Coulibaly et al. 2025.

Note: The dependent variable is the log of income in 2017 purchasing power parity dollars. FDP = forcibly displaced person; IDP = internally displaced person.

plays a significant role in fostering social relations, and by extension in maintaining long-term economic and social activity, it may be prudent for hosts to favor established economic relationships over new and potentially temporary ones, resulting in discrimination against FDPs (Betts 2021; Greif 1993; Sahlin 1972). To disentangle these factors, two additional Oaxaca-Blinder decomposition were conducted.

First, to understand the potential importance of discrimination in determining refugees' incomes, the incomes of Nigerian refugees are compared to those of IDPs (figure 4.5). Because the two groups are hosted in the same location and face similar pressures as new arrivals, comparisons between them account for the potential impacts of location and latecomer effects, with any unexplained factors likely due to refugee discrimination. This analysis shows that the difference in income between Nigerian refugees and IDPs appears entirely as a consequence of endowment effects, with the unexplained component of the model statistically insignificant. Nigerian refugees and IDPs are treated similarly, if not equally, and differences in their incomes result from differences in endowments, not from discrimination.

Second, comparing the incomes of Malian refugees and IDPs reveals that 88 percent (0.71/0.81) of the differences in their income is due to unexplained factors. It could be due to discrimination against Malian refugees; however, given the absence of discrimination against refugees from Nigeria, a more likely explanation is that the poorer environmental conditions in the areas hosting Malian refugees have led to lower returns. This is because the overwhelming majority of IDPs in the Harmonized Survey on Households Living Standards 2018–2019 data set reside in areas hosting Nigerian refugees, not in areas hosting Malian refugees. Differences in location between IDPs and Malian refugees are thus captured in the model's unexplained component, which is likely driving the vast difference in income between the two groups.

This theory is supported by comparisons between the areas hosting Nigerian and Malian refugees. Nigerian refugees not only live in comparatively more fertile areas but demonstrate access to improved economic opportunities via the informal cross-border trade networks that exist with Nigeria, opportunities not available to Malian refugees (CBN 2016).[12]

Figure 4.5 Oaxaca-Blinder Decomposition of IDPs versus Nigerian Refugees and IDPs versus Malian Refugees, Niger

Difference in log income

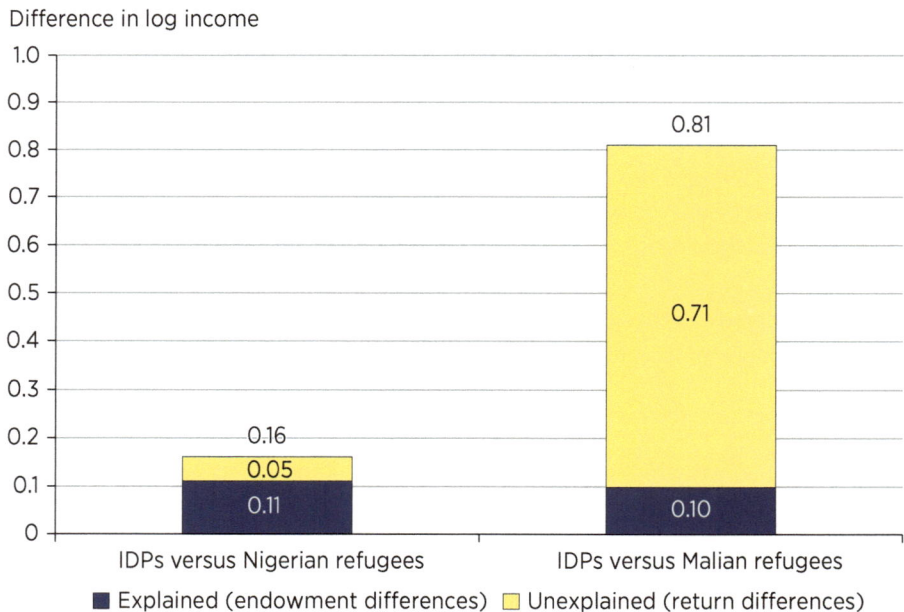

Source: Coulibaly et al. 2025.

Note: The dependent variable is the log of income in 2017 purchasing power parity dollars. IDP = internally displaced person.

Reflection: Importance of Dispersion and Portable Assistance

This vignette explores whether the rights assigned to refugees by Nigerien law are complied with in practice. The results provide cause for optimism and are sobering at the same time: optimism because, although Niger is one of the poorest countries in SSA, its progressive policies on refugees' economic inclusion contribute to levels of self-reliance not seen elsewhere on the continent, with the difference in self-reliance between hosts and refugees smaller than anywhere else in the region. Furthermore, not only are Niger's refugee-hosting policies progressive, but this vignette also finds no evidence of labor market discrimination against foreigners, with refugees from Nigeria performing on par with IDPs in Niger.

The results remain sobering nonetheless: poverty levels among FDPs remain high and their degree of self-reliance, by extension, low. Without ample humanitarian support to FDPs, which they currently do not receive in Niger, one expects those who are displaced and who have lost productive capacities to go through a period of hardship in the country. Even when endowments are restored to their original levels, returns may be lower because of "latecomer effects," with the most attractive parcels of land and economic opportunities already taken. Comparisons between Malian refugees and IDPs suggest a different explanation for these adverse outcomes: restricted economic opportunities. This explanation is most evident for Malian refugees who live in areas with limited soil fertility and few opportunities for trade. A recent analysis from the World Food Programme and UN Refugee Agency (UNHCR) confirms that in northern Tahoua and Tillaberi, where most Malian refugees live, poor natural endowments significantly impede Malian agricultural activity (WFP and UNHCR 2023). All Malians (100 percent) in Tahoua and 63 percent in Tillaberi reported poor soil quality as a major constraint on their agricultural production, compared to just 46 percent of Nigerian refugees living in Maradi and Diffa, highlighting the importance of geography in determining refugees' outcomes (WFP and UNHCR 2023).

Among refugees from Nigeria, who reside in areas where farming is more feasible, few engage in agricultural activity, even though self-employed farming is the more remunerative activity. Furthermore, many Malian refugees opt to remain in infertile areas with limited economic opportunities, despite having freedom of movement; instead, they settle in peri-urban areas where their skills are less in demand. The reasons are not entirely clear, but results presented in this vignette are at least compatible with the suggestion that the availability of humanitarian support in certain (peri-urban) locations leads FDPs to cluster in informal settlements near these areas, as opposed to dispersing across rural locations. Consideration of the locations where refugees have settled, and where UNHCR provides support—including through the construction of housing and financial support to schools, clinics, and public infrastructure—suggests a spontaneous process of clustering. Doing so is rational for refugees and humanitarian agencies, because it creates efficiencies in the provision of assistance while allowing refugee households to survive displacement. In the long term, however, it impedes self-reliance: more lucrative economic activities, such as agriculture, remain inaccessible, because agriculture can be successfully practiced only in areas of low population density, not in the peri-urban zones where assistance is being provided (refer to the Uganda vignette). The provision of location-based humanitarian assistance thus leads refugees to seek employment in other sectors for which they are less equipped, while creating dependence on humanitarian assistance. If this reasoning has validity (and similar arguments were made for Uganda), refugee self-reliance in Niger should improve if humanitarian support to refugees shifts from place-based (in-kind) provisions to portable cash-based support.

Kenya: The Challenge of Ending Large-Scale Encampment

As of April 2025, Kenya hosted about 850,000 refugees and asylum seekers. The vast majority of Kenya's refugees live in camps (86 percent), with just 14 percent in urban areas, predominantly Nairobi. Refugee camps have been present in Kenya for over 30 years. Dadaab camp, located in the northeast of Kenya near the Somali border, is by far the largest, hosting nearly one-half of the country's refugee population. The next largest camps or settlements are Kakuma and Kalobeyei in Kenya's remote northwestern region of Turkana, which combined host nearly 300,000 refugees and asylum seekers. Until February 2022, when Kenya's 2021 Refugees Act became effective, refugees were officially not allowed to live outside camps and were denied the right to own cattle, cultivate land, move freely, work, or integrate with local people, rendering them entirely dependent on humanitarian assistance. The new act paves the way for socioeconomic integration by granting refugees the right to work, freedom of movement in a designated area, and the right to own property, offering the potential to move away from dependence on humanitarian assistance toward self-reliance.

As Kenya's refugee situation became increasingly protracted, the sustainability of strict encampment policies that kept refugees reliant on aid was inevitably questioned, leading to the serious exploration of alternative strategies designed to promote refugee self-reliance. A key pillar of this approach has been the integration of refugees and host communities, accompanied by investments in area-based development. This was the approach adopted in the Kalobeyei Integrated Social and Economic Development Programme, commonly known as the Kalobeyei Initiative. Built just 3.5 km from Kakuma refugee camp, and opened in 2016, Kalobeyei was created as an integrated settlement, intended for both refugees and members of the host community (Betts 2021). The initiative introduced a range of innovative market-based mechanisms with the aim of promoting refugee self-reliance. These mechanisms include cash-based programs to meet housing, nutritional, and other material needs; specific training to support refugees and host community entrepreneurship; and programs to support dryland agriculture, including through household kitchen gardens (Betts 2021). They were accompanied by a regional development plan for the whole of the subcounty of Turkana West, covering both refugee camps and the surrounding areas.

The more recent Shirika Plan builds on the principles and framework established through the Kalobeyei Initiative. Many details of the plan remain as yet undetermined, but already Kenya's refugee camps have been converted into integrated settlements with municipal status. Within them, refugees enjoy many of the same rights as Kenyans, including freedom of movement and liberty to work or start a business. The expectation is that duplication in service provision will be eliminated as refugees transition from humanitarian-provided services to publicly provided services, and that self-reliance among refugees will be strengthened through the socioeconomic integration of refugees and host communities.[13] The Shirika Plan is accompanied by two area-based development plans—the Kalobeyei Integrated Socioeconomic Development Plan 2023–2027 and the Garissa Integrated Socioeconomic Development Plan 2023–2027—that are intended to strengthen the economies of these remote host areas.

This vignette explores some of the challenges associated with this model and with promoting refugees' economic inclusion following a protracted period of encampment. It also identifies potential interventions to improve refugees' integration and successful dis-encampment.

Benefits of Economic Inclusion

Before turning to the challenges associated with transitioning from large-scale encampment to economic inclusion, it is worth summarizing existing evidence on the economic impact of refugees' integration, particularly the seminal "'Yes' in

My Backyard" report (Sanghi, Onder, and Vemuru 2016). The authors of that report use computable general equilibrium simulations to analyze three scenarios for the two camps in Turkana: (1) ending encampment and moving refugees out of the country; (2) integrating skilled refugee labor into Kenya's economy while unskilled refugees remain encamped, although both refugee types continue to receive the same levels of transfers; and (3) integrating all refugees into Kenya's economy, where they continue to receive the same levels of transfers.

At baseline, the study notes that encamped refugees have become an integral part of Kakuma's social, cultural, and economic fabric, with many refugee-owned businesses serving both refugee and host communities. It finds that the presence of refugees has an overall beneficial and permanent impact on Turkana's economy, boosting the county's gross regional product by over 3 percent, increasing local employment by approximately 3 percent, and raising the per capita income of hosts by about 0.5 percent per year. Despite the positive average impact, the authors also observe significant heterogeneity in their findings. Activities in nontradable sectors benefit from the presence of refugees, but those in tradable sectors do not. When comparing outcome indicators across households with different income sources (small enterprises, wages, and agricultural and animal sales), the results show that the wage-earning and farming households of Kakuma observed growth in their assets, whereas those that sell animals observed a decrease. Although on balance the presence of refugees is associated with greater material well-being, this is not necessarily the case for mental well-being, with men reporting more "worries" than women, as do the middle-aged and the elderly.

Simulating the effects of further integration in the Kenyan economy shows large effects in the transition year, which become more muted over time (table 4.4). This trend is expected as economies adjust to "shocks" and eventually return to their equilibrium state. Results demonstrate how the presence of camps contributes to the economy in Turkana, with the dis-encampment scenario mostly showing negative effects on gross regional product, employment, and local income per capita. They also show that economic integration would raise gross regional product and the average income for local people, an effect that is greater with full integration. This work also points to significant distributional consequences from refugees' integration: employment for hosts declines because of increased competition, with the prices of nontradables falling as a result. These effects are largest in the short run but dissipate with time as the economy adjusts.

Table 4.4   **Macroeconomic Effects on Turkana, Kenya, under Three Scenarios**

Scenario	Transition year	+5 years	+10 years	+15 years	+20 years
		Gross regional product			
		(Percentage change from initial equilibrium)			
Integrate skilled only	4.7	0.1	−0.3	−0.4	−0.4
Full integration	15.1	0.3	−2.1	−2.7	−2.8
Removal of refugees	−2.6	−3.3	−3.3	−3.3	−3.3
		Employment (locals only)			
		(Percentage change from initial equilibrium)			
Integrate skilled only	−0.8	−1.2	−0.8	−0.6	−0.5
Full integration	−3.6	−7.0	−5.2	−3.9	−3.3
Removal of refugees	−1.2	−2.7	−2.8	−2.8	−2.8
		Gross regional income			
		(Percentage change from initial equilibrium)			
Integrate skilled only	0.8	−1.6	−1.1	−0.7	−0.6
Full integration	2.3	−5.3	−4.7	−3.9	−3.3
Removal of refugees	−2.6	−3.3	−3.3	−3.3	−3.3
		Gross regional income per local person			
Integrate skilled only	1.6	−0.5	−0.3	−0.2	−0.1
Full integration	6.1	1.9	0.5	0.0	−0.3
Removal of refugees	−1.4	−0.6	−0.5	−0.5	−0.5
		Nontradable prices			
Integrate skilled only	2.3	−0.6	−0.8	−0.9	−1.0
Full integration	7.1	−3.5	−5.3	−6.3	−6.5
Removal of refugees	−10.3	−6.8	−6.5	−6.5	−6.5

Source: Sanghi, Onder, and Varalakshmi 2016.

A second, partial equilibrium background study for this report considers the impact on refugees' incomes and self-reliance that may follow from the full economic integration of refugees into Kenya's economy (Hoogeveen, Leander, and Nsababera 2024). That paper decomposes income gaps between refugees and hosts across locations. Refugees in camp areas appear able to earn similar incomes as those of hosts with similar levels of education and experience. The analysis highlights the greater potential to earn incomes (for hosts and refugees) in an urban setting like Nairobi relative to the more isolated settings of Kakuma/Kalobeyei and Dadaab. Even if encamped refugees were fully economically integrated in the areas where they live now, their incomes would not change much because hosts are very poor as well. A more effective approach to promoting refugee self-reliance may be to allow greater geographic mobility, so refugees can move to areas with more abundant employment opportunities and higher economic returns, as illustrated using this report's measure of refugee self-reliance: self-earned income (figure 4.6).

The authors of that paper use an Oaxaca-Blinder decomposition to examine what is driving the within-group income differences for hosts and refugees between camp and urban areas. The study finds that, for refugees, differences in endowment explain only 11 percent of the income gap. In other words, no substantial differences arise in education, age, or other observable factors that explain the observed differences in income between urban and rural areas. Rather, the observed difference in earnings is attributable to better market

Figure 4.6   Self-Reliance for Refugees and Hosts, by Location, Kenya

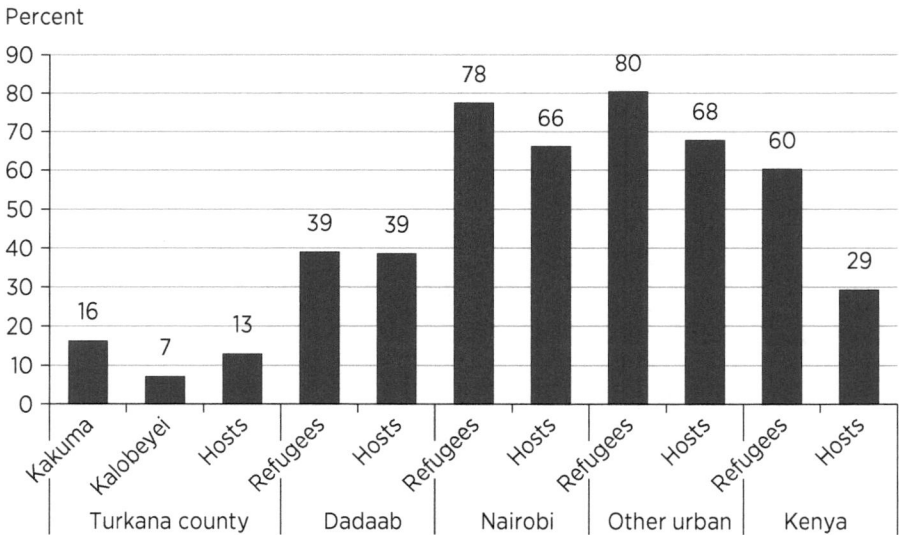

Source: Original calculations using data from the Kenya Longitudinal Socioeconomic Study of Refugees and Host Communities, 2023.

conditions in urban areas (that is, higher wages for similar work) or to unobservable differences between urban and camp-based refugees (for example, entrepreneurial spirit, work ethic, and so on). Among hosts, by contrast, differences in endowment account for 50 percent of the income gap between hosts in urban and camp areas. This finding suggests that hosts in rural areas would not necessarily be able to achieve the same level of income as urban Kenyans if they decided to migrate, potentially making it less attractive for them to move.

Will the Shirika Plan Increase Refugee Self-Reliance?

A limitation of the two studies discussed in the previous subsection is that they assume refugees' integration within Kenya's wider economy, yet the Shirika Plan does not envision such integration. It aims to transform the camps in municipalities to reduce legal barriers to economic inclusion through policy reforms associated with financial inclusion, documentation, and land tenure, and at the same time confine refugees to areas near the camps. The idea is that transforming camps into municipalities and giving refugees full economic rights within them will create new opportunities for income generation.

Figure 4.7   Employment for Hosts and Refugees around Camps, Kenya

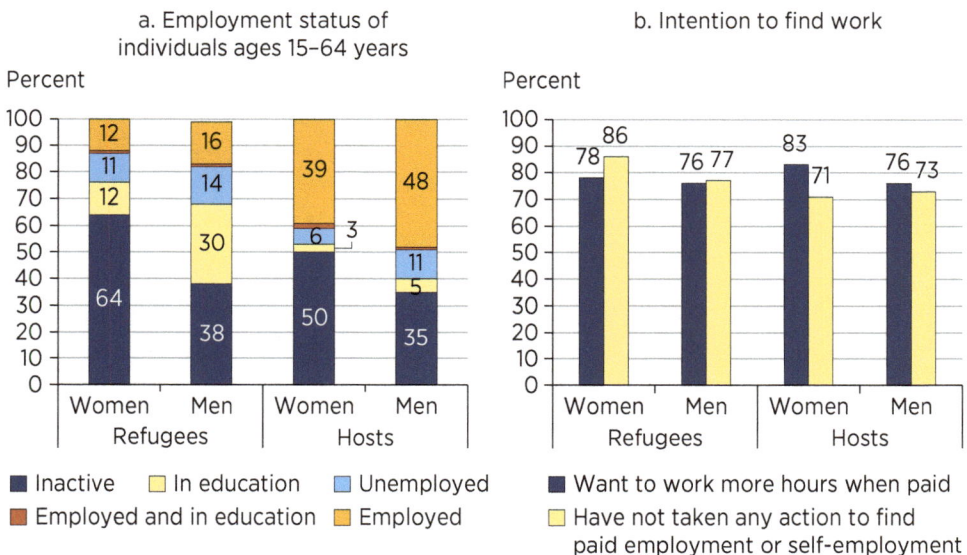

a. Employment status of individuals ages 15–64 years

b. Intention to find work

Legend (panel a): ■ Inactive   ☐ In education   ☐ Unemployed   ■ Employed and in education   ■ Employed

Legend (panel b): ■ Want to work more hours when paid   ☐ Have not taken any action to find paid employment or self-employment

Source: Adapted from the Kenya Longitudinal Socioeconomic Study of Refugees and Host Communities, 2023.

How likely is it that the greater availability of (refugee) labor around the camps will lead to increased income generation? The microeconomic simulation suggests that refugees' incomes would not change much, and the effect on the host population is left unanswered. In the abstract, economists would argue that a greater availability of labor (a resource) creates a depressing effect on wages, which makes it more attractive for entrepreneurs to invest and create jobs. In addition, fewer restrictions should promote refugees' entrepreneurship and increase self-employment. In practice, the size of both effects is likely to be small. Data from the Kenya Longitudinal Socioeconomic Study of Refugees and Host Communities 2023 help illustrate why.[14] As figure 4.7 demonstrates, (before Shirika Plan implementation) few refugees were employed and most hosts were not gainfully employed either. Although many refugees and hosts stated they want to work additional hours, most did not take any action to look for work, suggesting the existence of a labor surplus. The effect of even more surplus labor on prevailing wages is likely to be limited; with that limited effect, the employment-generating effect of lower wages diminishes significantly.

The scope for increased self-employment is limited as well. Refugee camps, and certainly those in Turkana, are found in the more marginal parts of Kenya, with restricted potential for gainful employment and economic activity. Local demand for goods and services is limited, because levels of poverty are among the highest in the country and population density among the lowest. Distances to consumer markets are large and costly to cover, the agropastoral economic potential is constrained by low rainfall and high temperatures, and the scope to develop a (dematerialized, online) service industry is hindered by language barriers, low levels of education among hosts and refugees, and inconsistent electricity supplies.[15] Thus, the often-heard argument that the legal transformation of camps into municipalities will increase economic activity is far from evident.

The view that the economic environment around the camps is not conducive to sustained economic development is echoed by Fellesson (2023) and by an International Finance Corporation study titled "Kakuma as a Market Place" (IFC 2018). Fellesson argues that the reason self-reliance in Kalobeyei is as limited as it is in Kakuma is that both are vested in an environment with few economic opportunities. The International Finance Corporation study notes how the vibrant business activity in and around the camps is driven by the humanitarian economy and warns that a combination of low levels of education and savings, lack of financial literacy, and limited access to outside markets due to poor road connections and the absence of a commercial airport creates major obstacles to market development. In fact, economic activity might possibly decline if the humanitarian camp economy winds down and leads to a fall in demand for local goods and services.

These arguments are supported by the 2009 World Development Report, which cautions against the notion that economic growth can be spread through area-based development (World Bank 2009). Its main message is that economic growth is typically unbalanced and that trying to spread it discourages it. Rather than bringing development to the people, the report suggests that people should move to where the activity is. In its view, development can still be inclusive, provided people who start their lives far away from economic opportunity benefit from the growing concentration of wealth in places like Mombasa or Nairobi. The way to combine the benefits of uneven growth with inclusive development is through economic integration; however, for areas with low population density, like Garissa and Turkana, the report warns that

> it does not make a lot of sense to spread expensive infrastructure into these places—or to give firms incentives to move to them. What makes much more sense is to provide basic services, even if it costs more to reach these distant areas. Encouraging mobility of people is the priority, and institutions that make land markets work better and provide security, schools, streets, and sanitation should be the mainstay of integration policy. (World Bank 2009, xxii)

Reflection: Making Dis-encampment Work

The Shirika Plan envisions area-based development to accompany the transition of camps into municipalities. Given that Garissa and Turkana counties are among the poorest in Kenya, increased investments in these areas are justified especially because, as figure 4.8 shows, the host population is in many respects worse-off than refugees. Additional spending on basic services, human capital development, and connecting these remote areas to the rest of the economy is much needed.

The government of Kenya is right to take a leaf from Uganda's playbook and consider hosting refugees as a potential vehicle for local development; however, whether area-based development will create sufficient economic opportunities to structurally promote refugee self-reliance is doubtful. For self-reliance to become a success, the strategy will need to include freedom of movement and the ability to settle elsewhere in the economy. Few would agree that integrating almost 900,000 refugees overnight in the economy is realistic or even desirable. Doing so would lead to congestion and overcrowded schools, create additional stresses on health facilities, and aggravate the already dire housing and sanitation conditions of many urban and rural residents. It is not a coincidence that the Shirika Plan speaks of a gradual process, but what might gradual economic inclusion look like, and how can it be successful?

Figure 4.8   Comparing Welfare Outcomes for Refugees and Hosts Living Near Camps, Kenya

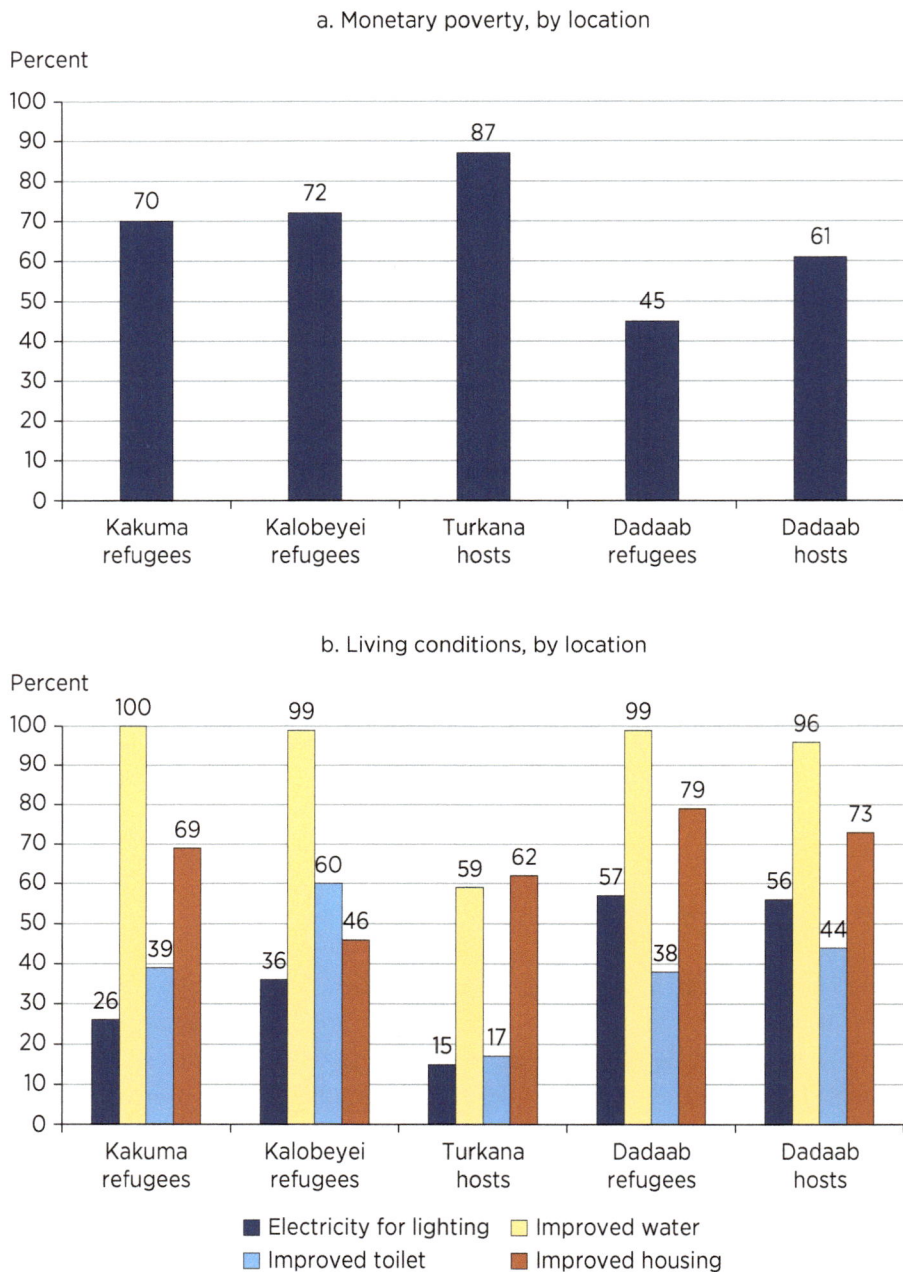

a. Monetary poverty, by location

Percent

b. Living conditions, by location

Percent

■ Electricity for lighting   □ Improved water
■ Improved toilet   ■ Improved housing

(continued)

Figure 4.8   Comparing Welfare Outcomes for Refugees and Hosts Living Near Camps, Kenya *(continued)*

c. Primary and secondary school enrollment, by location

Percent

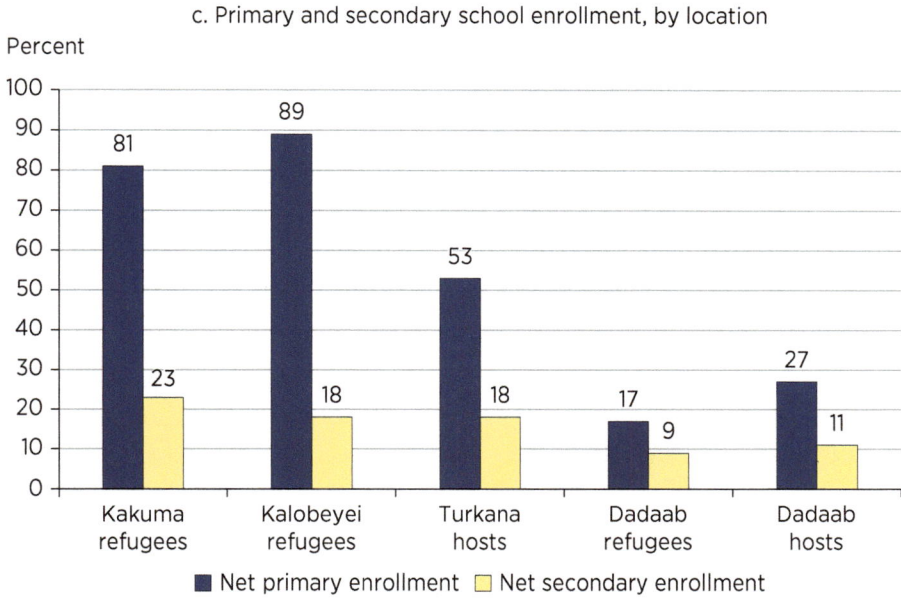

■ Net primary enrollment ☐ Net secondary enrollment

d. Quality of education, by location

Percent

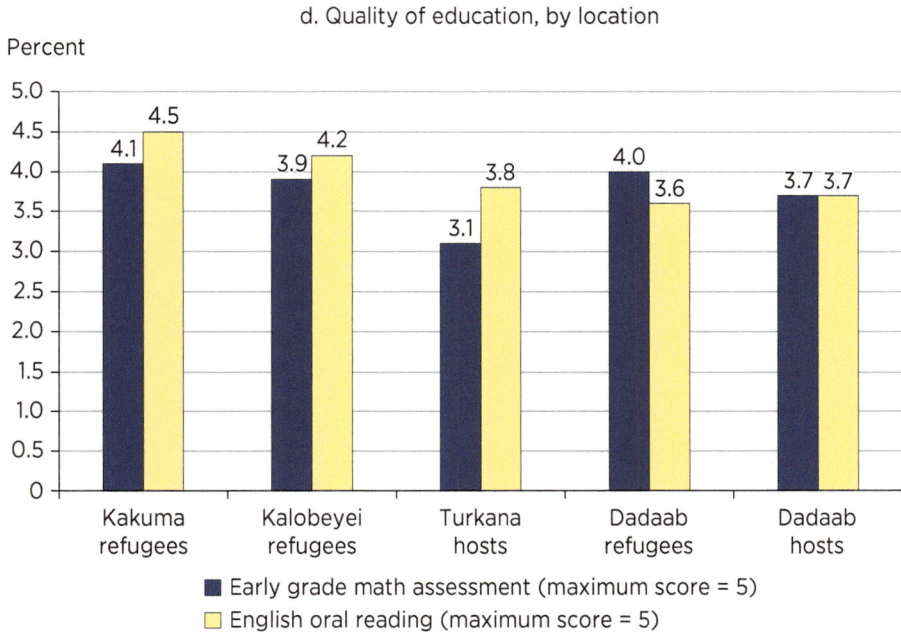

■ Early grade math assessment (maximum score = 5)
☐ English oral reading (maximum score = 5)

Source: Adapted from the Kenya Longitudinal Socioeconomic Study of Refugees and Host Communities, 2023.

At the outset, it should be clear that 900,000 refugees represent a large but not unmanageable number. Every year Kenya's economy grows by about 1 million people through natural growth, and, in 2022, Kenya's labor force increased by 750,000 young people (KNBS 2023a). Thus, incorporating encamped refugees in the economy over multiple years is comparable to accommodating a year of population and labor force growth. Moreover, many refugees are farmers and pastoralists (refer to figure 4.3), and may not seek to move to an urban center. Provided with access to land or livestock, these refugees could be interested in spreading out across the country and integrating into rural communities, which, in turn, may be interested in receiving refugees, especially when their arrival comes with investments in local service infrastructure, such as schools and clinics.

Dispersing refugees will be less daunting when it is a whole-of-government approach involving different line ministries in coordination with the Department of Refugee Services. For instance, prioritizing communities that express willingness to host refugees for planned investments in clinics; classrooms; water, sanitation, and hygiene facilities; and irrigation—essentially linking planned unconditional investments to refugees' reception—can encourage greater interest in hosting them and promote their more even distribution across the country.

If the government of Kenya has concerns about too large and too sudden an outflow of refugees to urban areas, it could set up a permit system that grants a certain number of refugees each year the irrevocable right to move freely around the country (in return for the obligation to permanently leave camp).[16] This system might not be necessary at all. The vignettes for Niger and Uganda suggest that the provision of humanitarian assistance and parallel service provision in certain locations, in combination with the cost and risks associated with moving, create a strong incentive to stay put. Depending on the assistance offered, many encamped refugees may be inclined to remain; however, this situation too might lead to concerns. If camps are transformed into municipalities and refugees become free to live in these areas, local congestion may arise when refugees who presently live in camps (where population density is as high as 11,000 people per km^2) settle elsewhere in the municipality, leading to negative local distributional impacts on nontradable markets, such as housing and employment.

Given these concerns, this report argues that adjusting the type of assistance provided is worth considering.[17] Rather than providing housing, other unconditional gifts, and incentive work to refugees, it would be attractive to level the playing field with hosts and introduce public works programs (PWPs) accessible to anyone (hosts and refugees) interested and able to work. Such programs, which should reduce in size over time, could aim to reduce the scope for conflict over resources and increase agropastoral potential by investing in land, water management, (re)forestation, and security. PWPs would thus, in addition to creating short-term employment, increase economic opportunities around camps in the long term, while (1) allowing hosts to deal with the potential negative distributional consequences on employment associated with refugees' integration, and (2) strengthening the skills and job-readiness of refugees.

Replacing assistance with PWPs for those able to work has the added advantage that the perverse incentives associated with the provision of free goods (in-kind aid) are avoided, which may have a depressive effect on the total number of refugees, reducing the number of potential opportunistic arrivals. Introduction of PWPs (a development initiative) would be a concrete way to ensure that assistance targets only the most vulnerable refugees who are unable to work. These refugees might even be encouraged to stay in the camps, especially if their clustering together enhances the efficiency of service provision and allows the delivery of specialized care. In this way, a clear distinction is made between refugees who have the capacity to become self-reliant—who are incentivized to leave and settle elsewhere—and the most vulnerable, who should be welcomed to remain.

Dis-encampment and granting refugees the right to work and to move freely across Kenya's territory raises two potential additional concerns. First, doing so might present a security risk. Second, such a model might make Kenya an attractive destination for refugees. At face value, the security argument seems less compelling because anyone with an East African passport is free to move and work in Kenya, including those from Somalia and South Sudan, who make up 80 percent of encamped refugees. An important reason why many refugees do not use this option is that they would have to give up their refugee status and, with it, access to humanitarian assistance. It is another illustration of how the present approach to providing assistance creates perverse incentives that hinder the implementation of durable solutions.

Whether the introduction of rights to work and to freedom of movement will make Kenya a more attractive destination for refugees is an empirical matter. Most refugees simply go to the nearest safe location (Iqbal 2007), so assistance modalities might not matter too much. To the extent that they do matter, a move away from a care and maintenance model toward one based on self-reliance might dampen the number of refugees. Presently, through their prolonged presence, Kenya's camps have become part of a refugee economy in which the presence of health and education services, as well as access to handouts, becomes part of a predominant livelihood strategy, with "people moving in and out of humanitarianism" (Jansen 2016, 163). This situation will likely change once a shift is made toward employment-based approaches. All this is to say that the benefits of such an approach are likely to outweigh these concerns.

Chad: A Refugee Compact to Realize the Triple Win

Since the outbreak of conflict in Sudan in mid-April 2023, hundreds of thousands of refugees have sought refuge in Chad. Despite living in an impoverished and predominantly rural nation, the people of Chad have exhibited remarkable solidarity and generosity, hosting 1.366 million refugees—equivalent to approximately 8 percent of the country's total population (figure 4.9). As of April 2025, this figure included approximately 680,000 recent arrivals from Sudan. This influx has placed considerable strain on Chad's resources, compelling authorities to navigate difficult decisions in balancing their commitment to supporting refugees with their responsibilities toward their own citizens. The response from the international community has been swift and substantial, helping to alleviate some of the immediate pressures.

Accommodating a large influx of refugees is not new to Chad. Since at least 2005 refugees have arrived from the Central African Republic (from which Chad hosts about 140,000 refugees), and in 2016 the country experienced a major increase in its refugee population when large numbers of refugees also arrived from Sudan. Seven years later, when the most recent refugee inflow from Sudan began, most refugees who had arrived in 2005 and 2016 were still in camps. Chad is thus dealing with both an immediate and a protracted refugee situation.

As the refugee situation in Chad became increasingly protracted, the government considered more sustainable approaches to hosting refugees, while acknowledging the limited prospects for voluntary and safe returns. Increasing the financial autonomy of refugees and reducing reliance on humanitarian assistance became the cornerstone of Chad's approach to refugees. This perspective is reflected in the application decree of Chad's Asylum Law, signed in 2023 (Republique du Tchad 2023). The law embraces the local integration of refugees, commits to avoiding settling refugees in permanent camps, and promotes self-sufficiency. It offers refugees the right to own land, to engage in formal employment and commercial activities, to move freely, and to access banking services. Even though economic inclusion is the stated policy objective, and is reflected in the National Response Plan to the Sudanese Refugee Crisis, it has yet to materialize. Almost all newly arrived refugees continue to live in camps, or "organized sites" as humanitarian agencies prefer to call them, with little evidence of onward movement.

This vignette explores the economic rationale for including refugees in local economies and the benefits it would bring to refugees, the international community, and the people of Chad, thus creating a triple win.[18] It also points to the challenges faced in making integration happen, and the importance of preparedness.

Figure 4.9   Refugees Present in Chad, 2002–25

Number of refugees

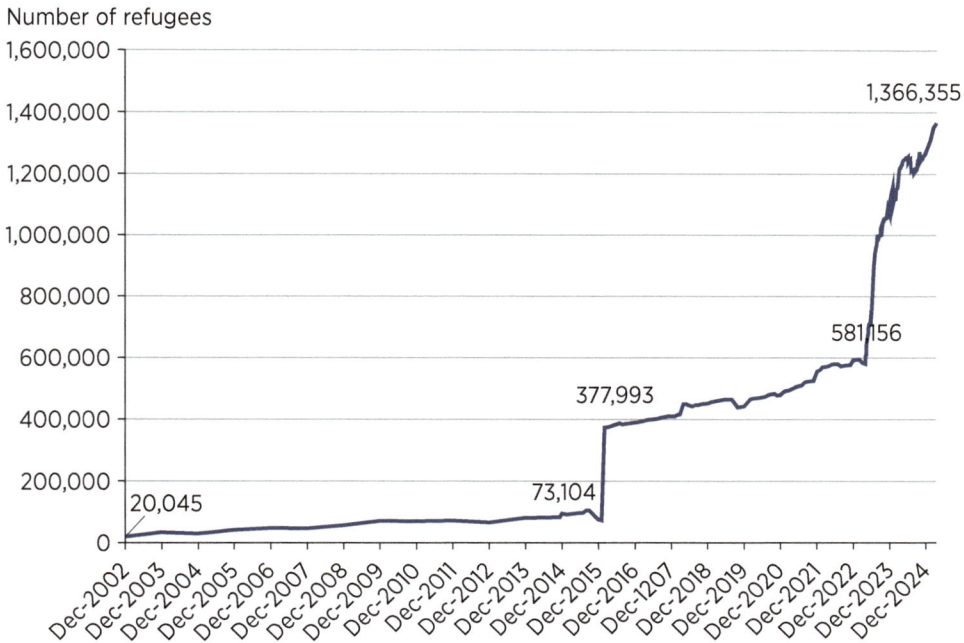

Source: United Nations High Commissioner for Refugees, Operational Data Portal, "Refugees in Chad," https://data.unhcr.org/en/country/tcd.

Note: Data from December of year indicated.

The Monetary Benefits of Refugees' Economic Inclusion

Chad is among the 10 poorest countries in the world, with a per capita income of $681 in 2023. The country is also one of the least urbanized in the world, with less than one-quarter of the population living in cities. N'Djamena is by far the largest urban agglomeration in Chad, with 1.6 million inhabitants, followed by the much smaller cities of Moundou and Sahr, each with less than 140,000 inhabitants.

Despite the country's progressive refugee policies, refugees in Chad live almost exclusively in camps strewn along the country's eastern and southern borders, where environmental conditions are harsh and economic opportunities few. The lack of opportunities around camps is reflected by the prevalence of poverty and low levels of self-reliance among both refugees and hosts. In 2018, 68 percent of refugees lived below the international poverty line and only 18 percent were self-reliant. Poverty is also extremely elevated (and self-reliance concomitantly low) in host communities (those living within a 15 km radius of camps), with an estimated 58 percent of hosts living below the international poverty line. This proportion is far higher than the national poverty rate of 31 percent, a number that itself is high and illustrative of both the country's widespread destitution (figure 4.10) and its limited economic means.

Figure 4.10 Poverty and Self-Reliance, Refugees, Hosts, and Overall, Chad, 2018 and 2022

Percent

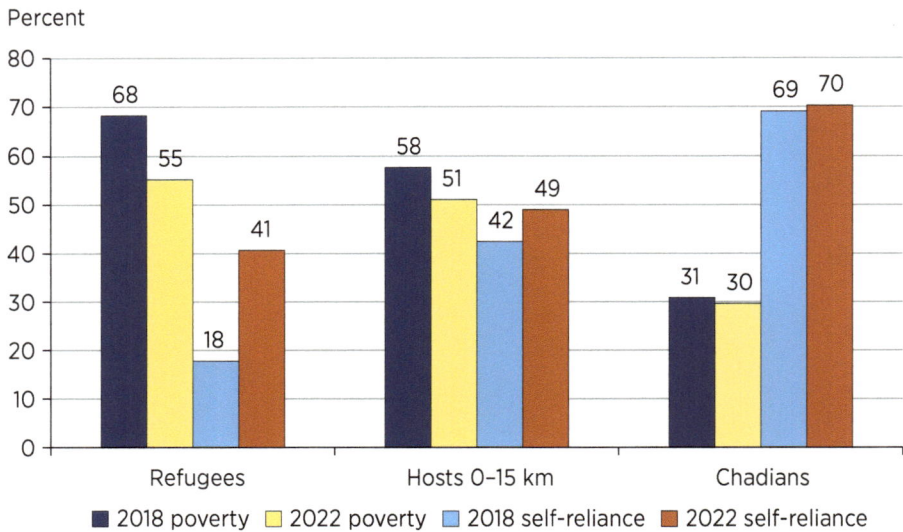

Refugees   Hosts 0–15 km   Chadians

■ 2018 poverty □ 2022 poverty ■ 2018 self-reliance ■ 2022 self-reliance

Sources: Original calculations and Coulibaly et al. 2025.

Between 2018 and 2022, a negligible reduction in poverty incidence occurred at the national level, with poverty falling by 1 percentage point to 30 percent and self-reliance increasing to 70 percent. Poverty among refugees, by contrast, reduced significantly over the same period, from 68 percent to 55 percent, a 13-percentage-point decline. Self-reliance rose even more impressively to 41 percent, a 23-percentage-point increase, driven by refugees in eastern Chad, with the situation for those in the south remaining largely unchanged (figure 4.11). Refugees living in areas with access to markets and those with fewer dependents and more wage- or self-employed members benefited the most.[19]

The decline in poverty and increase in self-reliance among refugees between 2018 and 2022 are mirrored by those among host communities, though their improvements are less significant; poverty among hosts fell by 4 percentage points, from 68 percent to 64 percent, and self-reliance increased by 4 percentage points, to 46 percent. Refugees were thus able to somewhat close the welfare gap with hosts between 2018 and 2022, though both continue to face elevated levels of poverty.

Figure 4.11   Self-Reliance, Subsistence Aid Received by Poor Refugees, and Humanitarian Funding, Chad, 2018 and 2022

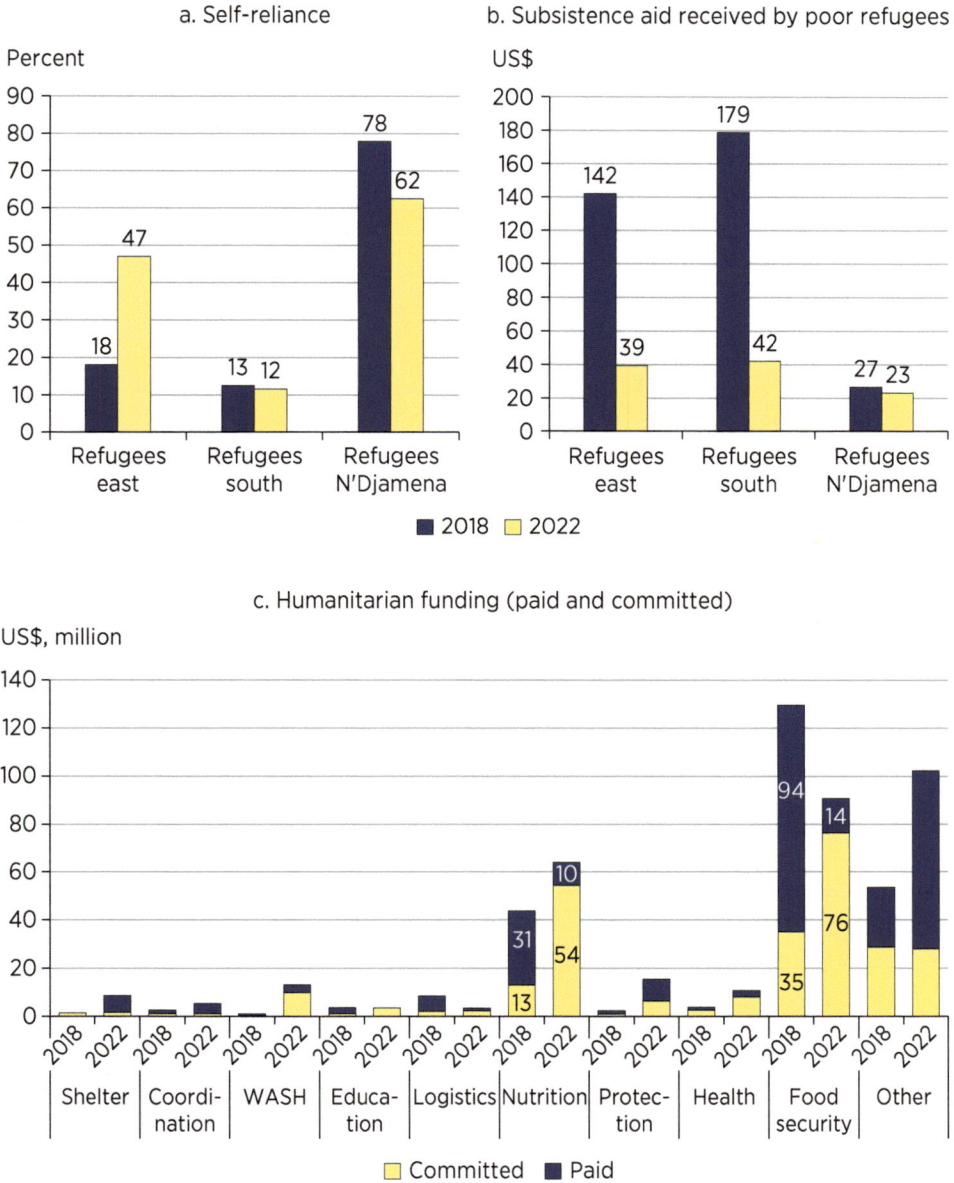

a. Self-reliance

b. Subsistence aid received by poor refugees

c. Humanitarian funding (paid and committed)

Sources: Self-reliance and subsistence aid received: original calculations and Coulibaly et al. 2025. Humanitarian funding: OCHA Services Financial Tracking Service (accessed January 4, 2025), https://fts.unocha.org/plans/1091/summary.

Note: WASH = water, sanitation, and hygiene.

Aid received by impoverished refugees fell sharply between 2018 and 2022, from an average of $148 per refugee per year to $39—an almost 75 percent decline. This decline was driven by an increase in the number of refugees (from 451,000 to 593,000) and a reduction in disbursed humanitarian resources, which declined from $163 million to $126 million.[20] Particularly sharp declines can be observed in the nutrition and food security categories, which fell by 80 percent, from $125 million in 2018 to $24 million in 2022. This decline is not in response to improved self-reliance, because refugees in Chad's south, whose self-reliance did not improve over this period, experienced a reduction in aid even larger than that experienced by refugees in the east, whose self-reliance improved. Refugees in the south thus experienced the double shock of declining self-earned incomes and a large reduction in aid, whereas refugees in Chad's east could compensate for a decline in aid through increased self-earned income.

Refugees staying in N'Djamena experienced smaller declines in aid, from $27 per refugee per year to $23 (figure 4.11, panel b). Therefore, by 2022, refugees residing in Chad's capital city were receiving aid comparable to that received by refugees in camps, putting them at odds with the patterns observed earlier in this report, which found that refugees living outside camps tend to receive less aid than those in camps. The reason for this equalization of benefits is that the benefits distributed to refugees in camps, who are more deprived than those in N'Djamena, were reduced, whereas those in the capital city were not. Before 2022, the pattern reported in chapter 2—that is, refugees outside camps receiving significantly less than those in camps—also held for Chad.

Reflection: The Case for a Refugee Compact

The refugee situation in Chad presents a strong case for establishment of a refugee compact. The country's high number of refugees and high level of poverty mean that refugees' economic inclusion will be difficult without significant external support. Nevertheless, various elements for a successful compact are already in place in Chad, which accommodates large numbers of refugees and has adopted liberal refugee policies. The large number of refugees and the country's low level of urbanization leave Chad susceptible to congestion and negative spillovers if too many refugees migrate to its urban spaces in a short span of time. Its vast territory, low population density, and availability of unused arable land[21] make land-based inclusion approaches a viable option for refugees' integration, especially given the refugee population's proclivity for agriculture.[22] Chad could, in fact, follow Uganda's lead and consider refugees' economic inclusion a vehicle for rural development by using refugee-related financing for investments in connectivity, markets, and service provision to the benefit of refugees and hosts alike.

Taking a financial perspective, panel a of figure 4.12 presents disbursed humanitarian aid along with a benchmark amount for subsistence needs required for refugees to meet a minimum acceptable standard of living if refugees are fully dependent and do not earn any income. This amount multiplies the number of refugees in the country with the international poverty line.[23] This benchmark thus covers spending on food, clothing, shelter, and other household essentials, but does not include expenses for critical services such as health and education.[24] The figure shows that, until the 2016 refugee crisis, disbursed humanitarian resources were sufficient to cover the full benchmark of subsistence needs in Chad, while leaving sufficient resources for necessary spending on health and education.[25] However, the availability of disbursed humanitarian resources barely changed over time, despite a quadrupling of the number of refugees in the country in 2016, leading inevitably to a steep decline in the resources available per refugee (figure 4.12, panel a). Although paid humanitarian resources expressed in per capita terms increased following the 2022 refugee emergency in the country, the available resources remain largely unchanged.

Figure 4.12   Paid Humanitarian Resources, Chad, 2004–24

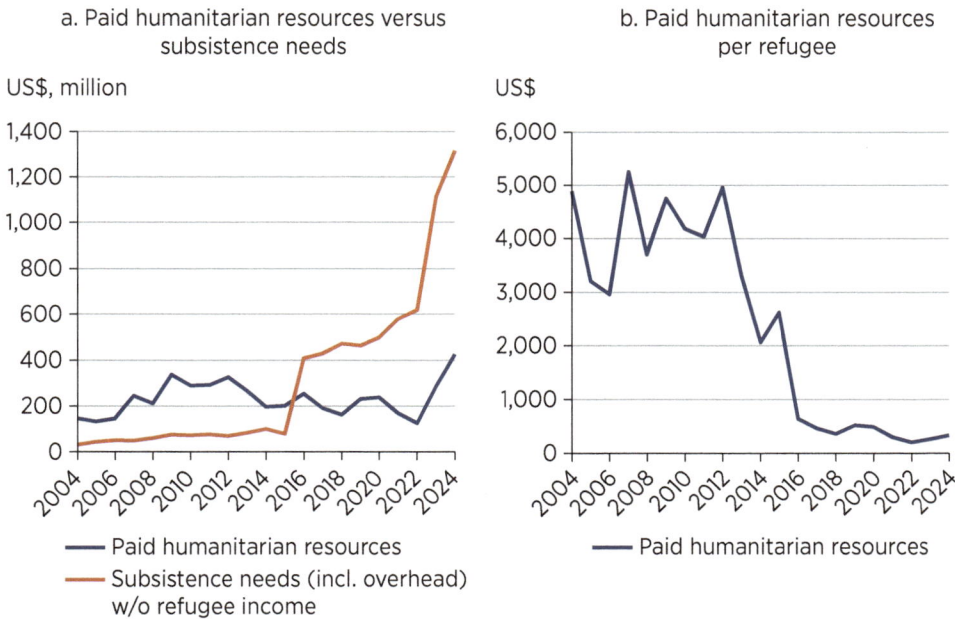

a. Paid humanitarian resources versus subsistence needs

US$, million

b. Paid humanitarian resources per refugee

US$

Paid humanitarian resources
Subsistence needs (incl. overhead) w/o refugee income

Paid humanitarian resources

Sources: Subsistence needs: original calculations. Paid humanitarian funding: OCHA Services Financial Tracking Service (accessed January 5, 2025), https://fts.unocha.org /plans/1091/summary.

As outlined in this report, the amount of humanitarian assistance needed by refugees depends on their ability to earn their own income. The benchmark subsistence needs referenced in the previous paragraph represent an implausible situation in which refugees do not work at all. Figure 4.13 presents a more realistic estimate of the potential cost of humanitarian needs by exploring two scenarios: one in which refugees earn as much as their hosts, and one in which refugees earn as much as encamped refugees in southern Chad.

The first scenario presents an optimistic view of what refugees might be expected to earn in the short to medium term. In 2022, existing encamped refugees in the east could almost attain this level of earnings, whereas refugees in the south were significantly poorer. The first scenario therefore presents an ambitious, but feasible, situation. The second scenario presents a more pessimistic view, assuming that newly arrived refugees experience few economic opportunities, comparable to what encamped refugees in Chad's southern region experience. In both scenarios, the cost of meeting subsistence needs is adjusted so that refugees are on average as well-off as their hosts (refer to the section in chapter 3 titled "Benchmark Cost of Subsistence Needs for Refugees in SSA"), thereby ensuring that after receiving assistance refugees are not better-off than the Chadian population. The costs also include an allowance for mistargeting and leakage. Both scenarios include the cost of integrated health and education services, assuming that refugees do not benefit from parallel humanitarian services but make use of publicly provided services.[26]

Figure 4.13   Disbursed Humanitarian Aid and Two Scenarios for the Cost of Hosting Refugees, Chad, 2004–24

US$, million

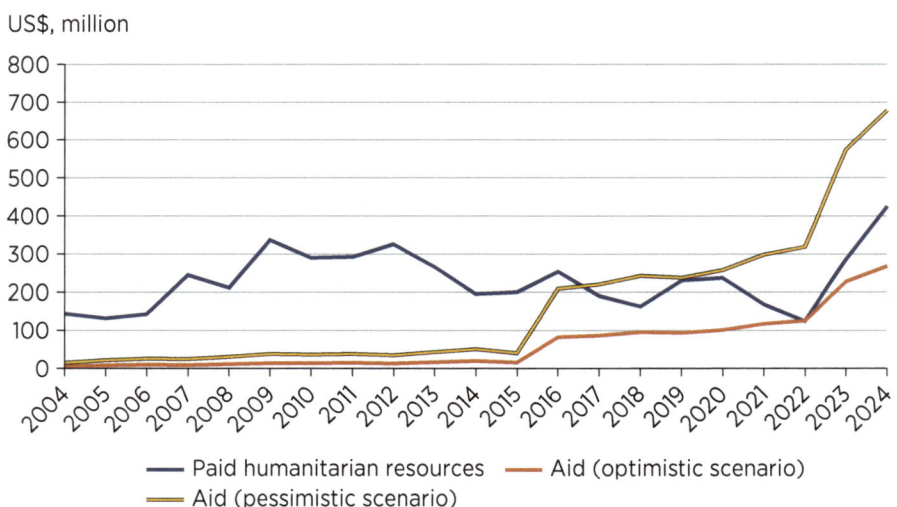

Sources: Aid: original calculations. Paid humanitarian funding: OCHA Services Financial Tracking Service (accessed January 5, 2025) https://fts.unocha.org /plans/1091/summary.

Figure 4.13 demonstrates that, despite the relatively low level of paid humanitarian resources, these resources can be adequate depending on the approach taken. If refugees' income-earning opportunities remain constrained (pessimistic scenario) more humanitarian resources than are presently provided will be needed (at least $679 million). In the absence of these resources, refugees will continue to experience high levels of destitution. If, by contrast, refugees are given adequate income-earning opportunities, and if they can make use of publicly provided services, then the cost of hosting refugees may become even less than what is presently available as humanitarian resources. If refugees could earn as much as their Chadian hosts, the amount needed in humanitarian aid would be about $269 million, a 60 percent reduction compared to the pessimistic scenario and over one-third less than the $426 million disbursed in 2024.

This illustration makes clear that a more cost-effective way of hosting refugees exists, one that allows refugees greater financial autonomy and dignity, and that can strengthen the national systems for health and education, as opposed to creating parallel humanitarian systems. This approach will also lead to the redistribution of limited resources by moving away from humanitarian handouts and toward productive investments in the development of host communities. Organized differently, Chad's humanitarian crisis has the potential to become a catalyst for local development to the benefit of refugees and hosts alike.

On Preparedness

Chad lies in a region affected by tension and conflict. In view of this context, it is important to move beyond a reactive, crisis-response approach to displacement and to focus instead on preparedness for events that can often, though not always, be predicted. For example, for eight years before 2024, the number of refugees in Chad gradually increased before rapidly rising in 2022 (figure 4.9), and, in 13 of the last 20 years, more than 10,000 refugees annually arrived in the country. Since 2014, this number has increased, with 7 of the last 10 years seeing more than 35,000 refugees arrive. The country has overcome an important hurdle with the adoption of inclusive refugee policies that promote the local integration and inclusion of refugees in national service provision, as well as that embrace refugee self-reliance. Realizing self-reliance and its benefits, however, will require promotion of dis-encampment and relocation of refugees across Chad's territory. Not only would dis-encampment help realize a triple win, but it is also likely the best way to prepare for the next refugee crisis, because many of the activities and capacities needed to dis-encamp successfully would be essential to respond to new inflows effectively.

To make this happen, the government of Chad, humanitarian agencies, and development actors could jointly consider a Chad Refugee Preparedness Compact that combines dis-encampment and increased preparedness with additional resources for investments in refugees' productive capacity and host communities' economic development. Other countries in the region have already signed similar compacts. Ethiopia's Jobs Compact matches development assistance for job creation in the country's industrial parks to the gradual relaxation of labor market controls for 30,000 refugees. Kenya's Shirika Plan links greater economic opportunities and freedoms for encamped refugees to area-based investments in the regions hosting camps. Chad's Refugee Preparedness Compact could equally link refugees' relocation and economic inclusion with local development initiatives for its host communities, thereby helping the country realize its objectives for refugees' integration, inclusive growth, and infrastructure development.

Notes

1. Primary data come from the Uganda Refugee and Host Communities Household Survey 2018. The survey is representative of the refugee and host populations in the Southwest and West Nile regions, and the city of Kampala. The host population is defined as the native population in districts where refugee settlements are situated.
2. Nonhumanitarian consumption can be equated to income earned by refugees if it is assumed that net savings are zero.
3. Nakivale, for instance, has only three settlement sites, of which the smallest, Juru, still has more than 30,000 people. The largest, Rubondo, hosts over 95,000 (UNHCR 2024b).
4. Refugee Economies, "Refugee Economies Programme: Dataset," https://www.refugee-economies.org/dataset.
5. United Nations High Commissioner for Refugees, Operational Data Portal, "Refugees and Asylum Seekers in Niger," https://data.unhcr.org/en/country/ner.
6. FDPs encompasses refugees, asylum seekers, other people in need of international protection, and IDPs.
7. The primary data source used in this chapter is Niger's Harmonized Survey on Household Living Standards 2018–2019, a nationally representative survey of over 6,000 households. A separate stratum collected information on refugee and IDP households in Diffa, Tahoua, and Tillabéri, the main host regions in Niger.
8. Industry refers to mining, quarrying, construction, water, electricity, and other industry. Services refers to transportation, hospitality, arts, and other services.
9. Using the International Labour Organization's definition of unemployment and data from Niger's Harmonized Survey on Household Living Standards 2018–2019, this chapter finds that the unemployment rate is about 0.7 percent for refugees, 1.2 percent for IDPs, and about 1.7 percent for hosts. According to that definition, an unemployed person is a person aged 15 or over who simultaneously meets three conditions: being unemployed for a given week; being available to take a job within two weeks; and having actively sought a job in the last four weeks or having found one starting in less than three months (ILO 2018).
10. Refer also to Famine Early Warning System Network (FEWS NET), "Kenya—Livelihood Zones," https://reliefweb.int/map/kenya/kenya-livelihood-zones.
11. Income is proxied by nonhumanitarian consumption.

12. International Monetary Fund, "Nigeria: Informal Trade with Neighboring Countries" (accessed April 23, 2024), https://www.imf.org/en/Data/Statistics/informal-economy-data/Reports/nigeria-informal-trade-with-neighboring-countries.

13. In line with efforts such as the Shirika Plan, UNHCR and the World Food Programme are working on a Differentiated Assistance Approach that weans better-off refugee households from humanitarian assistance by providing market-led solutions and skills for increased economic participation.

14. The survey was implemented in the areas of (1) Kakuma refugee camp, (2) Kalobeyei integrated settlement, (3) Dadaab refugee complex, (4) greater Nairobi, and (5) Mombasa and Nakuru. In the refugee camp areas, the survey also included host communities within 15 km of the camp borders. In urban areas, it included hosts living in neighborhoods where a large share of the urban refugee community resides.

15. Camps are located in areas of the country where destitution is highest. Whereas the average poverty rate in Kenya is 39 percent, it is 78 percent in Turkana County and 68 percent in Garissa County, putting both among the three poorest counties in the country (KNBS 2023b). Moreover, with population densities of less than 20 people per km^2, Turkana and Garissa are among the least densely populated counties in the country, in turn a reflection of the limited agronomical potential of these (semi-) arid areas, where pastoralism and animal husbandry remain the main sources of livelihood (FEWS NET, "Kenya—Livelihood Zones"). Betts (2021) acknowledges that, even though a market-based approach to self-reliance works better, refugees in Kalobeyei remain far from self-sufficient. As the Kenya vignette argued, this outcome is expected in view of the limited economic opportunities available in Turkana and the restrictions on freedom of movement.

16. Brazil implements a significant refugee relocation program, primarily focused on Venezuelan migrants arriving in large numbers through the northern states of Amazonas and Roraima, where they are then voluntarily relocated to other cities across the country with better integration opportunities, as part of an initiative called "Operação Acolhida" (Operation Welcome). In Mexico, a significant refugee relocation program exists whereby UNHCR actively moves asylum seekers and refugees from southern Mexico, where job opportunities are scarce, to central and northern cities with better economic prospects, providing them with support like housing, job placement, and access to social services to facilitate their integration into new communities; this program is referred to as the "Programa de Integración Local" (Ferris 2024).

17. Betts (2021) describes another interesting experiment of switching the assistance model from in-kind to cash-based. He describes the neighboring camps of Kakuma and Kalobeyei in northern Kenya: Kakuma follows the traditional model of providing mostly in-kind assistance, whereas Kalobeyei adopts a cash-based model built on refugee agency and market functioning. Thus, refugees in Kakuma receive a prefabricated shelter; those in Kalobeyei are offered money to construct their own. Refugees in Kakuma receive in-kind food assistance; those in Kalobeyei receive cash assistance and a kitchen garden. Evaluating the impact of the cash-based approach, results find it leads to higher calorie intake, improved food security, and better dietary diversity, as well as better self-reported well-being and independence from humanitarian aid. Refugees in both camps report similar levels of nonfood consumption, employment, and other key indicators. The main cause of the heightened welfare outcomes in Kalobeyei, according to Betts, is the different modes of assistance. In Kakuma, food rations led refugees to sell part of their assistance at a discounted price in order to purchase preferred items, whereas the cash assistance and kitchen plots in Kalobeyei meant refugees could purchase and produce their desired items without inflated transaction costs, improving food security and self-reported well-being and autonomy among recipients.

18. For its empirical work this vignette draws on data from the ECOSIT4 and ECOSIT5 surveys (Enquête sur la Consommation des ménages et le Secteur Informel au Tchad). The surveys, implemented in 2018 and 2022, were a collaboration between the National Statistics Office (Institut national de la statistique, des études économiques et démographiques) and UNHCR. The 2022 survey was completed just before the latest inflow of refugees from Sudan.
19. Based on regression analysis on entry and exit out of poverty using a panel of refugee households. The full analysis is available in Coulibaly et al. (2025).
20. The decline in the amount paid contrasts with the increase in the funded amount from $249 million to $317 million; the difference is due to commitments, which increased from $86 million to $191 million.
21. Approximately 40 percent of Chad's land area, equating to over 49 million ha, is classified as agricultural. As of 2018, however, only about 6 percent of this land was under cultivation, indicating significant untapped potential (World Bank 2018).
22. Seventy-eight percent of refugees from Sudan have a background in agriculture (UNHCR 2024c).
23. To be precise, it is the number of refugees times the annual value of $2.15 per day expressed in current purchasing power parity dollars, and includes an 8 percent overhead for administrative expenses.
24. For Chad, providing integrated services for education and health costs an estimated $24 million for education and $32 million for health (UNHCR and World Bank 2024a, 2024b; World Bank 2023).
25. This relative abundance of financing may explain why Nguyen, Savadogo, and Tanaka (2021), who used 2018 survey data on refugees living in camps, found that refugees had considerably better access to health and education services than host communities, and even better than the average Chadian.
26. In accordance with earlier estimates, the cost for mistargeting and leakage is set at 29 percent of the subsistence amount needed (including 8 percent administrative costs). The cost for integrated health and education services is estimated at 9 percent of the benchmark subsistence costs. The actual cost for assistance to refugees may be higher because it does not include certain provisions, such as for water, sanitation, and hygiene or coordination, yet these costs tend to be relatively minor (refer to, for instance, figure 4.11).

References

Atamanov, Aziz, Johannes Hoogeveen, and Benjamin Reese. 2024. "The Costs Come before the Benefits: Why Donors Should Invest More in Refugee Autonomy in Uganda." Policy Research Working Paper 10679, World Bank, Washington, DC.

Betts, Alexander. 2021. *The Wealth of Refugees: How Displaced People Can Build Economies*. Oxford University Press.

Bohnet, H., and C. Schmitz-Pranghe. 2019. "Uganda: A Role Model for Refugee Integration?" BICC Working Paper 2/2019. Bonn International Center for Conflict Studies, Bonn.

CBN (Central Bank of Nigeria). 2016. "Measuring Informal Cross-Border Trade in Nigeria." CBN, Lagos.

Center for Preventive Action. 2024. "Violent Extremism in the Sahel." *Global Conflict Tracker*, October 23, 2024. https://www.cfr.org/global-conflict-tracker/conflict/violent -extremism-sahel.

Coulibaly, Mohammed, Johannes Hoogeveen, Robert Hopper, and Aboudrahyme Savadogo. 2025. "Towards More Sustainable Solutions for the Forcibly Displaced in Niger." Background paper for *Making Refugee Self-Reliance Work: From Aid to Employment in Sub-Saharan Africa*. World Bank, Washington, DC.

Fellesson, Måns. 2023. "A Sustainable Solution or Just a Different Form of Humanitarian Assistance? Examining the Kalobeyei Integrated Socio-Economic Development Plan (KISEDP)." *Refugee Survey Quarterly* 42 (2): 158–79. https://doi.org/10.1093/rsq /hdad001.

Ferris, Elizabeth. 2024. "Refugee Relocation Can Be a Positive Experience." Edward P. Djerejian Center for the Middle East Issue Brief, Rice University's Baker Institute for Public Policy.

Greif, Avner. 1993. "Contract Enforceability and Economic Institutions in Early Trade: The Maghribi Traders' Coalition." *American Economic Review* 83 (3): 525–48.

Hoogeveen, Johannes, Sebastian Leander, and Olive Nsababera. 2024. "Unpacking Spatial Variations in Refugee Self-Reliance in Kenya." Background paper for *Making Refugee Self-Reliance Work: From Aid to Employment in Sub-Saharan Africa*. World Bank, Washington, DC.

IFC (International Finance Corporation). 2018. "Kakuma as a Market Place. A Consumer and Market Study of a Refugee Camp and Town in Northwest Kenya." IFC, Washington, DC.

ILO (International Labour Organization). 2018. "Measuring Unemployment and the Potential Labour Force in Labour Force Surveys: Main Findings from the ILO LFS Pilot Studies." ILO, Geneva.

Iqbal, Zaryab. 2007. "The Geo-Politics of Forced Migration in Africa, 1992–2001." *Conflict Management and Peace Science* 24 (2): 105–19.

Jansen, Bram J. 2016. "Digging Aid: The Camp as an Option in East and the Horn of Africa." *Journal of Refugee Studies* 29 (2): 149–65.

KNBS (Kenya National Bureau of Statistics). 2023a. "Quarterly Labour Force Report: Quarter 4 October–December 2022." KNBS, Nairobi.

KNBS (Kenya National Bureau of Statistics). 2023b. *The Kenya Poverty Report. Based on the 2021 Kenya Continuous Household Survey*. Nairobi: KNBS.

Nguyen, Nga Thi Viet, Aboudrahyme Savadogo, and Tomomi Tanaka. 2021. "Refugees in Chad: The Way Forward." World Bank, Washington, DC.

Republique du Tchad. 2023. "Decret No. 0648/PT/PM/MATDBG/2023." N'Djamena. https:// www.ecoi.net/en/file/local/2091861/645b938a4.pdf.

Sahlin, Marshall. 1972. *Stone Age Economics*. New York: de Gruyter.

Sanghi, Apurva, Harun Onder, and Varalakshmi Vemuru. 2016. "'Yes' in My Backyard? The Economics of Refugees and Their Social Dynamics in Kakuma, Kenya." World Bank, Washington, DC. http://documents.worldbank.org/curated/en/308011482417763778.

UNHCR (United Nations High Commissioner for Refugees). 2023a. "Uganda Refugee Operation—Impact of Underfunding in 2023 (September to December)." UNHCR, Geneva. https://data.unhcr.org/en/documents/details/104366.

UNHCR (United Nations High Commissioner for Refugees). 2023b. "Global Survey on Livelihoods and Economic Inclusion, 2023." UNHCR, Geneva. https://www.unhcr.org /sites/default/files/2023-11/global-survey-on-livelihoods-and-economic-inclusion -report.pdf.

UNHCR (United Nations High Commissioner for Refugees). 2024a. "Niger January 2024 Operational Update." UNHCR, Geneva. https://data.unhcr.org/en/documents /details/106742.

UNHCR (United Nations High Commissioner for Refugees). 2024b. "Uganda Refugee Statistics December 2024 Settlement & Urban Profiles." UNHCR, Geneva. https://data .unhcr.org/en/documents/details/113643.

UNHCR (United Nations High Commissioner for Refugees) and World Bank. 2024a. "The Global Cost of Refugee Inclusion in Host Countries' Health Systems." World Bank, Washington, DC.

UNHCR (United Nations High Commissioner for Refugees) and World Bank. 2024b. "Economic Participation and the Global Cost of International Assistance in Support of Refugee Subsistence Needs." World Bank, Washington, DC.

WFP (World Food Programme) and UNHCR (United Nations High Commissioner for Refugees). 2023. "UNHCR/WFP Joint Assessment Mission in the Regions of Diffa, Maradi, Tahoua, Tillabéri – Niger 2022." UNHCR, Geneva. https://microdata.unhcr.org /index.php/catalog/945#doc_desc.title_statement.

World Bank. 2009. *World Development Report 2009: Reshaping Economic Geography*. Washington, DC: World Bank.

World Bank. 2018. "Chad: World Bank Grants $41 Million to Promote Adoption of New Agricultural Technologies and Boost Productivity." Press release, April 30, 2018. https://www.worldbank.org/en/news/press-release/2018/04/30/chad-world-bank -grants-41-million-to-promote-adoption-of-new-agricultural-technologies-and -boost-productivity.

World Bank. 2019. "Informing the Refugee Policy Response in Uganda: Results from the Uganda Refugee and Host Communities 2018 Household Survey." World Bank, Washington, DC.

World Bank. 2023. "Developing a Methodology for Measuring the Impact of Hosting, Protecting and Assisting Refugees (Phase II) The Global Cost of Inclusive Refugee Education: 2023 Update. " World Bank, Washington, DC.

CHAPTER 5

Toward Greater Refugee Self-Reliance in Sub-Saharan Africa

Introduction

The current refugee response model is under significant strain. With refugee numbers rising, humanitarian funding dropping, and the care and maintenance model of refugee assistance limiting self-reliance, a shift in approach is needed. A more effective and sustainable long-term strategy would be to focus on increasing refugees' income through improving their economic opportunities. Higher incomes would enhance refugees' financial autonomy and reduce their reliance on humanitarian aid.[1] Savings could then be invested in the development of host countries, creating a triple-win scenario that benefits refugees, humanitarian agencies, and host governments and communities alike.

Chapter 3 estimated that increasing refugees' incomes by 25 percent could reduce the need for humanitarian assistance by $900 million. If these resources are used for investments in host communities and channeled through government systems, host governments would automatically assume a greater role in the refugee response. As the vignettes in chapter 4 illustrate, however, achieving greater refugee self-reliance is not simple, and many challenges are associated with refugees' economic inclusion.

This final chapter examines various factors that need to be considered when the objective is to enhance refugee self-reliance. It identifies key bottlenecks in the transition to a sustainable self-reliance model and outlines essential actions for host countries, humanitarian agencies, and development actors, whose interlinked efforts are crucial to this endeavor. A better equilibrium can be achieved only if all stakeholders play their part, including, of course, refugee and host communities, the first to be affected by any changes in a refugee-hosting regime.

Aligning the Responsibilities of Host Countries and Humanitarian Agencies

Many refugee responses, particularly in Sub-Saharan Africa (SSA), take on a transactional shape—one in which host countries provide asylum and land, and humanitarian agencies in turn provide care and maintenance to refugees. However, as demonstrated in previous chapters, this approach is inefficient and unsustainable: scarce resources are spent on refugees who are willing and able to care for themselves, and refugees' outcomes on self-reliance remain unsatisfactory long after the emergency phase.

An alternative model is feasible—one in which host countries bear the primary responsibility for promoting refugee self-reliance and humanitarian agencies support emergency response (in the immediate onset of a crisis) and legal protection of refugees (until the forced displacement situation is resolved). Such a division of roles is observed in Europe and Latin America, but much less so in SSA, where humanitarian agencies continue to provide noncritical services long after the emergency phase. Rethinking these roles is important.

Such a response model is premised on host government leadership. Host governments can introduce policies that promote refugee self-reliance and reduce the financial and social costs of hosting refugees. These policies include access to labor markets and freedom of movement—rights that tie in with inclusion in national service provision as well, because refugees will be reluctant to move to where they can find jobs if they cannot also access local health and education systems there. With inclusion in labor markets and national service provision, the need for parallel systems disappears, and humanitarian agencies can focus on emergency response and the advocacy and protection of refugees' legal and human rights.

Like many reforms across sectors, moving from parallel systems to refugees' inclusion introduces changes to the status quo, including shifts in roles and responsibilities (refer to annex 5A). These changes can create opportunities for improved collaboration and partnerships between government, development, and humanitarian actors. However, inclusion inevitably means reducing the role of actors involved in parallel systems and increasing the responsibilities of relevant line ministries and government agencies. Such shifts need to be managed carefully to mitigate risks related to perceived competition over resources and policy influence.

Perceptions of host communities will have to be managed as well to avoid negative attitudes toward refugee inclusion. Approaches that invest in host communities that welcome refugees, or approaches that redirect refugee financing into public service provision or improvements for the benefit of hosts and refugees, can positively influence support for refugees' inclusion (Baseler et al. 2024).

With inclusion in national systems, other aspects align as well. Humanitarian standards, for instance, tend to be higher than national standards; however, once refugees are integrated in national systems, refugees and hosts are treated the same. That is not to say, however, that the system should lower standards for refugees. Instead, once refugees attain the same standards as host populations, any additional investments should be directed to increasing the overall standards for both refugees and hosts.

Adapting Financing and Investment Models to Self-Reliance

Development partners engage with refugee self-reliance through two channels: (1) the financing they provide to host governments for refugee situations; and (2) the interventions they support either directly or indirectly by channeling resources through humanitarian agencies.

This funding architecture is associated with several inconsistencies. The mismatch between using humanitarian funding to address protracted situations has already been observed, as was the fact that countries with approaches that limit self-reliance (for instance, by hosting refugees primarily in camps) increase refugees' dependence and with it the need for assistance and financing. Consequently, a country that adopts more inclusive refugee policies that contribute to greater refugee self-reliance may, under the current system, find that financing for refugees drops. Moreover, as long as financing for refugee situations is tied to services provided by humanitarian agencies, host countries face the impossible choice of either leaving the handling and management of refugees largely to humanitarian agencies or taking charge of refugees themselves, including the financing.

A more sustainable approach separates financing of refugee situations from the provision of services, with financing channeled to host governments that then decide whether to provide services themselves or to engage outside agencies to do so on their behalf. With nearly all encamped refugees in SSA (99.8 percent) residing in International Development Association (IDA) or IDA-blend countries (figure 5.1), significant opportunity exists to align development financing with reduced encampment and the promotion of self-reliance.

Figure 5.1   Percent of Encamped Refugees in SSA, by Host Country Lending Category, 2024

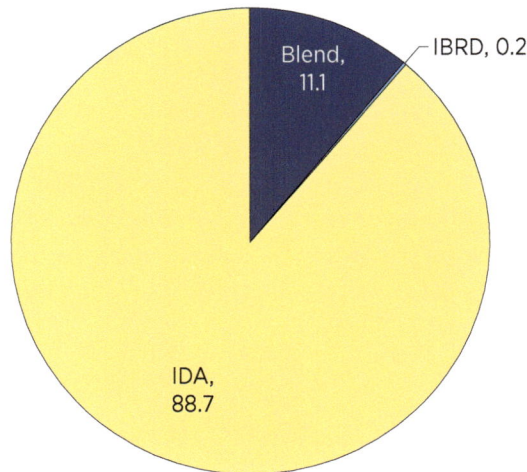

Blend, 11.1

IBRD, 0.2

IDA, 88.7

Sources: UNHCR 2025; World Bank, World Development Indicators, 2024 (accessed February 27, 2025), https://datatopics.worldbank.org/world-development-indicators/the-world-by-income-and-region.html.

Note: IBRD = International Bank for Reconstruction and Development; IDA = International Development Association; SSA = Sub-Saharan Africa.

The transition to greater refugee self-reliance would be facilitated not only by channeling financing through host governments but also by more predictable financing that aligns with the core objective of economic inclusion. Needs-based financing does not meet this criterion, because the need for assistance increases with reduced access to economic opportunities. A rule-based allocation system, by contrast, takes into account aspects like the wealth of a country (high-income countries have less need for financial burden sharing), the number of refugees, the protractedness of the situation (emergency situations are expensive), the prevailing refugee policy framework, and the economic opportunities provided to refugees.

At present, financial allocations demonstrate seemingly random variations in support for refugees. Chapter 3 demonstrated that assistance received by refugees varies between as well as within countries, with variations that reflect neither the degree of refugees' destitution nor the policy environment. The amount of official development assistance provided per refugee varies from $1,042 in South Sudan to $286 per refugee (over two years) in Sudan, with the amounts unlikely to reflect differences in the degree of poverty experienced by refugees in those countries. Financing also does not reflect the economic opportunities extended to refugees: the Democratic Republic of Congo receives 10 percent more per refugee than neighboring Uganda, even though Uganda's policies are far more progressive (figure 5.2).

Figure 5.2   ODA per Refugee, Largest ODA Recipients in SSA, 2020–21

US$

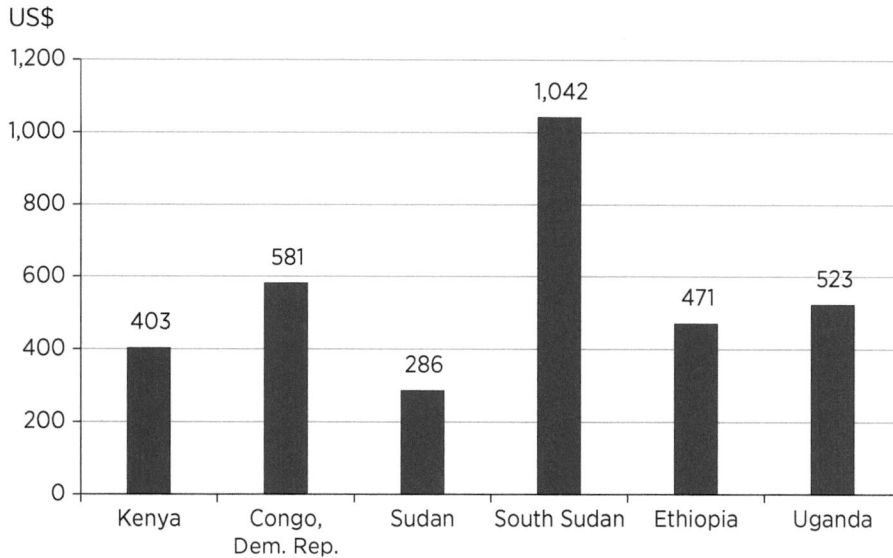

Sources: Original calculations using OECD 2023 and UNHCR 2023.

A well-designed, rule-based system of allocation for refugee assistance is more transparent, avoids hard-to-explain differences, and incentivizes economic inclusion. Its assistance is based less on needs and better reflects the provision of economic opportunities to refugees. Such a sophisticated funding mechanism may seem hard to achieve—and is certainly a deviation from the present system—but development financing has been allocating resources through such a mechanism for many years, with IDA allocations based on population size, the degree of economic development,[2] and an assessment of the quality of policies and institutions in eligible countries. IDA allocations essentially prioritize countries with greater need (based on population) and better policies for receiving larger funding allocations. With rule-based allocations feasible for development financing, they should also be feasible in refugee situations.

At the country level, aligning financing with the inclusion of refugees in national systems might be relatively straightforward, because the recurrent cost per refugee can be easily estimated. It has already been done for inclusion in health and education in the largest refugee-hosting countries (UNHCR and World Bank 2024; World Bank 2023). These estimates are based on average public spending per student or per patient. Financing instruments that compensate host governments for services delivered, such as P4R (Program-For-Results) projects, could then be used to reimburse host governments for results achieved, leading to payments against the number of refugee children in school, of refugees who accessed public health services, and of those who benefited from national social protection programs.[3]

As such, an important role that host governments can play is to advocate for results-based development financing by catalyzing triple-win compacts, such as the Emergency Preparedness Compact proposed in the Chad vignette in chapter 4, the Ethiopia Jobs Compact, or Kenya's Shirika Plan. Such compacts can ensure coherence among host government, humanitarian agencies, and donors.

On the investment side, development agencies can support host governments in their transition to greater self-reliance through support with legal and policy reforms, building sectoral capacity to accommodate refugees in national systems, designing monitoring systems, investing in host communities, and developing policies to foster a more dynamic economic environment that can better absorb refugee inflows. Not all these activities have to be newly designed. Development agencies can incorporate refugees in current project designs, as they do for other vulnerable groups. Thus, when new classrooms are planned in an education program, one allocation criterion could be whether the village has (or will include) refugees in its schools. Public works programs can be planned where refugees (intend to) settle and can offer employment opportunities to hosts and refugees. In this way, development programs can help with the dispersal of refugees and promote local integration at the same time.

Although advocacy for humanitarian financing remains important, recent announcements point to a significant decline in external funding and fiscal pressures among key donors suggest an increase is unlikely in the coming years. An option to explore is whether part of the available humanitarian grant funding could be channeled through multilateral development banks. By leveraging grants, these banks can transform the grants into much more voluminous (now subsidized) loans, thereby alleviating financing constraints. For most low-income countries in SSA, this option would not bring significant changes: under the prevailing multilateral development bank financing rules, most low-income countries remain eligible for grant financing. Such funding would, however, be channeled through government systems rather than through parallel humanitarian systems. For middle-income countries, transforming grants into concessional loans implies that far larger amounts of financing can be made available. Because governments tend to prioritize their own citizens, it is essential that financing for refugees—whether in the form of loans or grants—is additional to country allocations for development financing.

Breaking the Curse of Encampment

Almost three-quarters of all refugees in SSA (74 percent) live in camp or camp-like settings (refer to figure ES.3 in the executive summary). Despite public commitments to the opposite, many new refugees, such as those from the Sudan crisis, live in newly created or existing camps and settlements. As outlined in chapter 2, however, encamped refugee households are less likely to be self-reliant and are far more likely to receive a disproportionately high share of humanitarian assistance.

The limitations of camp-based approaches have long been recognized. A decade ago, the UN Refugee Agency (UNHCR) published its "Policy on Alternatives to Camps," explaining that "camps can have significant negative impacts over the longer term for all concerned," including through "distort[ing] local economies and development planning, while also causing negative environmental impacts" (UNHCR 2014, 4). That policy paper called for encampment to "be the exception and, to the extent possible, a temporary measure" while advocating for "camps to be phased out at the earliest possible stage" (UNHCR 2014, 6). In 2018, UNHCR's Head of Communications reiterated that message, discouraging encampments and calling for "settlements [to be] built that are completely integrated with the local community" with the intention of "attract[ing] international development assistance as well as private investment" (Betts 2021; UNHCR 2018, 24). In 2024, UNHCR reaffirmed its commitment to phasing out camps in its paper on "Sustainable Programming," which emphasizes the importance of refugees' integration and the need to "avoid setting up camps to the maximum extent possible" (UNHCR 2025, 3).

Several countries in SSA—including Rwanda, South Africa, Somalia, and Togo—have committed to avoiding the establishment of (new) refugee camps or settlements. Others, such as Zambia, have begun transitioning away from traditional refugee camps to integrated settlements. Despite this positive shift, the fact remains that, a decade after UNHCR published its "Policy on Alternatives to Camps," most refugees in SSA are still in camps or camp-like settings (refer to box 5.1 for more on camps over time).

The vignettes in chapter 4 highlight some of the key challenges associated with ending encampment. They demonstrate the persistent attraction of camps during emergencies, as well as the challenges of closing (large) camps once they have emerged. As seen in Niger and Uganda, even where inclusive refugee policies exist, most refugees continue to live in camp-like situations that are not conducive to self-reliance. Camps create their own justification for existence through a circular chain of actions that start with the desire to assist desperate and vulnerable people during an emergency, and end with a situation in which refugees are cared for, but are dependent on this care. Once camps are established, refugees, humanitarian agencies, and host governments have incentives to stick with the current model of encampment and resist change.

From refugees' perspective, as long as their economic opportunities remain limited and humanitarian aid is offered to those in camps and not, or less so, to those living elsewhere, a strong incentive arises to remain encamped.[4] The Uganda vignette suggests that, even when more remunerative opportunities exist elsewhere, refugees who are trapped in poverty and unable to bear the cost (and risk) of leaving the camp-like situation in which they find themselves may be unable to access those opportunities.

From a host government's perspective, encampment may be attractive too. For cash-strapped governments, encampment has the advantage of keeping the financial responsibility of caring for refugees with the international community. Encampment in remote locations may also limit the impact of refugees on host communities and prevents refugees from settling elsewhere in the country, where they may create congestion[5] or engender security concerns.

For humanitarian agencies, encampment brings its own advantages. During emergencies, it allows for the rapid delivery of aid. When refugees arrive in remote parts of a country where bureaucratic capacity is limited or where national systems for health, education, and social protection are under stress, encampment offers an alternative to strengthening national systems.

Given these considerations, it is not surprising that encampment is entrenched in the refugee response model and that successful dis-encampment has remained largely elusive. Inevitably, breaking the curse of encampment and increasing refugee self-reliance require addressing various complementary factors, which can be derived from the vignettes in chapter 4. Relevant actions can be summarized as follows: (1) avoid encampment of new refugees by taking a policy stance against the creation of (new) camps, investing in preparedness, and supporting freedom of movement; (2) prevent negative spillovers by ensuring refugee inflows are dispersed and investing in locations where refugees settle; (3) strengthen refugees' ability to settle outside of camps by ensuring that assistance to vulnerable refugees is portable and not place-based; (4) agree on a transition plan at the onset of a crisis to gradually wind down temporary camps while building government capacity to provide basic services; and (5) create a conducive environment for refugees' inclusion by changing the financing model to one that is multiyear, predictable, and compatible with economic inclusion and that puts host governments in charge.

Box 5.1   Refugee Camps over Time

The African Refugee Camp and Settlement Dataset tracks all refugee camps and settlements in Sub-Saharan Africa since 1999, recording their location, date of creation and closure, and size (Anti, Salemi, and Rigberg 2025). Its data show that new camps continue to be created although some do close, which is encouraging and suggests that dis-encampment is feasible.

Since 2011 the total number of camps has increased, driven by large camps (those with 10,001 to 50,000 refugees) (figure B5.1.1). The number of very large camps (with over 50,000 refugees) has increased steadily. These increases are concerning, as is the limited number of small camps, which were common in the 2000s. Larger camps—which offer very limited options for self-reliance, particularly agriculture-based self-reliance—rarely get closed (only Ethiopia closed some following security concerns).

Figure B5.1.1   Number of Refugee Camps in SSA, by Size, 1999–2024

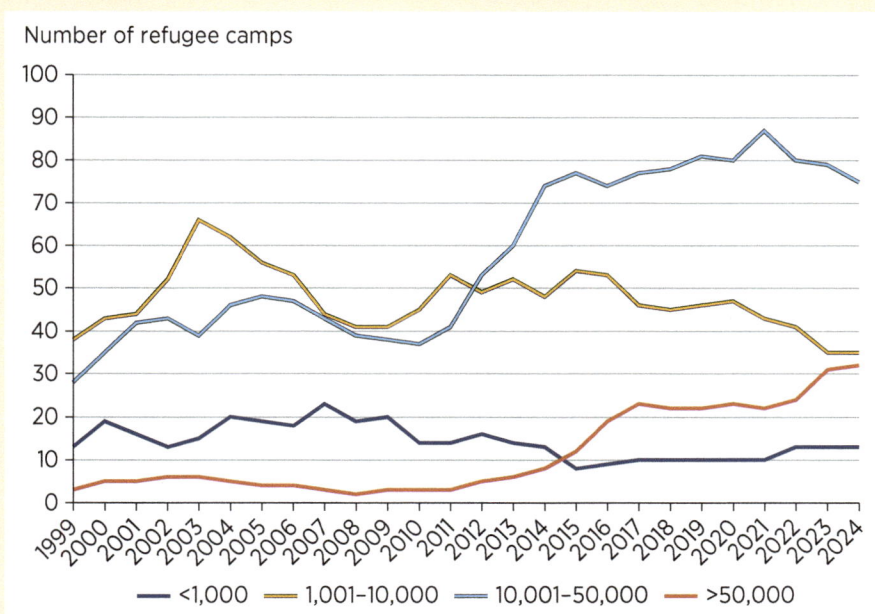

Source: Anti, Salemi, and Rigberg 2025.

Note: SSA = Sub-Saharan Africa.

Strengthening Refugees' Economic Inclusion

A critical step toward strengthening refugees' economic inclusion is to ensure the relevant policies are in place and enacted (figure 1.7 in chapter 1 suggests that a gap often remains between refugees' de jure rights and their de facto realization; refer also to Zetter and Ruaudel 2016). Table 5.1 presents an overview of essential policy dimensions taken from the World Bank's Refugee Policy Review Framework, with the following key elements: (1) ensure access to economic opportunities; (2) guarantee that other constraints, such as the need for identification and access to health and education services, are addressed; and (3) ensure adequate attention is paid to avoid negative spillovers on host communities.

Once a country has critical policies enabling self-reliance in place and is determined to pursue refugees' economic inclusion, it should encourage refugees to benefit from these opportunities. In doing so, the fallacy of refugees' dependence should be avoided. Instead, it should be recognized that refugees have agency and make informed choices. They can decide for themselves where economic opportunities exist and how to attain them, and do not need a bureaucracy to decide for them where to live, in what kind of house, how to get there, or in what activity to engage. Instead of having a shelter constructed for them, refugees should be trusted to be capable of constructing their own or of renting one. Rather than having land prepared for them, refugees should be trusted to be able to find land to rent themselves. Of course, refugees may lack the financial means to realize the opportunities they find for themselves, so they may need support during this transitional period to prevent them from becoming (poverty) trapped.

Some refugees may need more than financial support. Refugees who have been inactive for prolonged periods have lost critical labor market skills. Human capital that was valuable at home may be less valuable in a new environment. Social isolation and trauma may have diminished their ability to work. Skills mismatches are likely to hold people back; for instance, farmers may need to acquire new knowledge of local environments. Language barriers may render skills in trade and services less valuable, and educational qualifications may not be fully recognized in the host country. The various ways in which refugees' labor market success is inhibited also offer ways of overcoming these challenges (Desiderio 2016). Skills can be upgraded through training, traumas treated, and new languages learned. Not every labor market disadvantage will need to be overcome through interventions, because many nationals are affected by similar challenges. The task is to ensure that extended assistance is used selectively for the most vulnerable refugees only.

Table 5.1 Policy Dimensions Relevant for Refugees' Economic Inclusion

Policy dimension	Subdimension	Priority orientation
Host communities	Support for communities in refugee-hosting areas	Support is provided to refugee-hosting areas as part of an approach that takes into consideration the estimated socioeconomic impacts on local communities hosting refugees (1) in public resource allocations and (2) in extending social protection to individuals affected economically by the situation.
	Social cohesion	Effective steps are taken to identify, prevent, and mitigate social tensions and risks of violence between and within refugee and host communities, and to combat discrimination.
	Environmental management	Effective measures are in place to prevent or mitigate environmental degradation in refugee-hosting areas and sustainably manage natural resources.
	Preparedness for refugee inflows	Robust preparedness plans are in place to mitigate the impact of possible new refugee inflows.
Regulatory environment and governance	Normative framework	Policies related to refugee status determination, legal status, and rights and obligations of refugees are clearly defined and in line with applicable international and regional norms and standards; and are easily accessible and well known by refugees, the national and local authorities, and other national stakeholders.
	Security of legal status	Legal stay arrangements are secure and predictable with adequate time perspectives, and no expulsion of asylum-seekers or refugees takes place in violation of international law.
	Institutional framework for refugee management and coordination	An efficient government-led coordination system is in place and enables the management of the refugee situation, policy development, and effective coordination across government and with external parties. This system includes a representative consultation mechanism that allows the authorities to get input and feedback from refugees on decisions affecting them.

(continued)

Table 5.1 Policy Dimensions Relevant for Refugees' Economic Inclusion (*continued*)

Policy dimension	Subdimension	Priority orientation
	Access to civil registration and documentation	All refugees have access to official personal identification (proof of legal identity) and are able to register vital events (birth, marriage, divorce, and death) with the civil registry and be issued with documentation.
	Justice and security	Refugees enjoy a level of security on an equal basis with nationals; and refugees have access to civil, administrative, and criminal justice, and other grievance redress mechanisms under the same conditions as nationals.
Economic opportunities	Freedom of movement	Refugees can choose their place of residence and move freely across the country as nationals of a foreign country generally in the same circumstances would.
	Rights to work and rights at work	Refugees have access to the labor market, including by starting a business and seeking wage-earning employment, in the same way as nationals; and refugees enjoy protection of workers' rights on the same level as nationals.
	Land, housing, and property rights	Refugees can purchase, lease, and use housing, land, and property in the same way as nationals, without restriction on location, type, or duration, or at least benefit from the most favorable treatment accorded to nationals of a foreign country in the same circumstances.
	Financial and administrative services	Refugees have effective access to financial services and to administrative services (driving license, recognition of professional/academic qualifications, skills development) that are essential for economic opportunities.

(continued)

Table 5.1 Policy Dimensions Relevant for Refugees' Economic Inclusion *(continued)*

Policy dimension	Subdimension	Priority orientation
Access to national public services	Education	Refugees have the possibility to effectively and safely access the national education system under the same conditions as nationals.
	Health care	Refugees have the possibility to effectively and safely access the publicly financed health care system under the same conditions as nationals.
	Social protection	Vulnerable refugees and vulnerable host community members have access to basic levels of assistance in a manner that is equitable in terms of coverage, targeting, and levels of benefits.
	Protection for vulnerable groups	Protection and care are available to unaccompanied and separated children, refugee victims of trafficking in persons, survivors of gender-based violence, and other refugee groups with specific needs.
Cross-sectors	Gender	Refugees of all gender groups do not experience specific gender-related barriers to accessing services and economic opportunities.
	Social inclusion	All refugees—irrespective of their age, gender, race, ethnicity, religion, nationality, country of origin, statelessness, political opinions, indigenous status, disability, sexual orientation, membership in a particular social group, or other characteristics—benefit on an equitable basis from relevant policies, including those related to access to services and economic opportunities.

Source: World Bank, n.d.

Ensuring a conducive environment requires addressing the negative distributional effects associated with refugees' economic inclusion. The impact of additional refugee labor on competition in the labor market may be negligible if the economy is dynamic and growing, and if refugees are spread across the country; however, the impact may be substantial if refugees are confined to one specific location with few opportunities to begin with (as is the case for most camps). Some spillovers diminish over time as economies adapt: increased demand for consumer goods and housing will be followed by a supply response. Addressing other spillovers—such as environmental degradation, overcrowded schools and health facilities, or shortages in housing—will require investments.

Investing in the Preparedness Agenda

Host governments, humanitarian agencies, and donor partners must invest in preparedness, particularly by strengthening state capacity to integrate refugees into national systems. Although this concept may seem abstract, governments closing refugee camps are already putting it into action by building the institutional infrastructure needed to incorporate refugees into their economies.

Refugee movements are often presented as "crises"—unforeseeable events that require emergency responses. Although there are instances of sudden and unexpected refugee flows, many refugee situations follow a pattern.[6] In some cases, the build-up is slow, but it does not take much to predict that flows will increase if circumstances in the country of origin remain unchanged or worsen.

The most effective approach is to engage with countries of origin through diplomatic, security, and development efforts to address the root causes of fragility, conflict, and violence. Although these efforts can yield positive results, they are not always successful. When they fall short, host countries face the challenge of providing refugees with international protection while minimizing negative impacts on their own populations. This is where a preparedness agenda becomes crucial.

Such an agenda can build on experiences in other areas, for example in natural disasters. A shift from response to preparedness has occurred in this area over the last couple of decades: construction codes have been amended so that buildings do not collapse as easily, emergency teams have been trained to respond faster, and systems have been built to respond to crises. For instance, Ethiopia's Productive Safety Net Program finances public works in drought-affected regions, with the program growing—or shrinking—depending on where and when the drought is most severe.

What might a preparedness agenda for refugee shocks look like? For humanitarian actors, it is already under way: positioning food and nonfood items near potential refugee situations, developing rosters of personnel ready for rapid deployment, and establishing systems to call for funds immediately following a crisis. Host governments and their development partners must begin thinking along similar lines, because several steps can be taken before refugee flows materialize. These steps include the following:

- Adjust rules for fiscal transfers from central to local levels of government to ensure that municipal and local authorities can quickly access funding when new refugee populations arrive. Doing so enables authorities to provide housing, manage increased waste, and expand health and education services efficiently in line with rising demand.

- Prepare to deploy civil servants and other public sector employees to receiving areas so that such deployments can be smooth and immediate, for example, to immunize incoming populations.

- Strategically plan for the settlement of large populations across the country, because relocation becomes challenging once people have established themselves. Poorly chosen locations can lead to social tensions and increased costs due to the lasting impact of initial settlement decisions.

- Implement hosting policies that are both socially and financially sustainable, recognizing that most refugee situations persist for years, and often decades.

Concluding Reflection: Leadership and Dialogue Are Key to Refugee Self-Reliance

What should be evident at the end of this report is that the case for refugee self-reliance is strong. Promoting self-reliance is the humane thing to do: it enhances the dignity of refugees and strengthens host governments and their economies. Refugee-hosting governments and communities are well aware of these arguments and embrace them, as do humanitarian and development agencies.

Nevertheless, refugee self-reliance remains elusive in SSA. This report highlights some key, if self-evident, findings. If their ability to work is restricted, refugees will not be able to take care of themselves; when refugees receive tiny pieces of land, they will not be able to live off of them; if assistance is given in certain locations, refugees will flock to them; successful economies cannot be built in remote, arid areas; and refugees' dependence implies aid money has to be spent on care and maintenance rather than on development. These things may be obvious, but they reflect standing practice.

What can be done to promote self-reliance more successfully? This report identifies critical actions under five broad headings: (1) strengthening refugees' economic inclusion; (2) supporting host communities; (3) breaking the curse of encampment; (4) adapting financing and investment models; and (5) investing in a preparedness agenda. These key elements, discussed in detail throughout this report, are summarized in figure 5.3 and elaborated in annex 5A. Successful implementation requires the collective efforts of host governments, humanitarian agencies, and developmental actors.

Leadership is key to a successful transformation away from a care and maintenance approach. Host governments need to take charge of the refugee response—refugees are, after all, in their countries and host government actions will drive the welfare of refugees, as well as that of the host population. Once they have an inclusive policy environment in place, governments can take a strong policy stance against encampment or can work with humanitarian partners on dis-encampment strategies. They can advocate for triple-win compacts that invest in economic development, expand national public service provision to refugees, and address any negative spillovers associated with refugees' integration. They can clearly demarcate the roles and responsibilities of partners that operate within their borders. Finally, they can ask the international community to stand in solidarity with the refugee response by providing multiyear, flexible, and predictable financing based on self-reliance outcomes.

For their part, humanitarian agencies may require operational rewiring to focus on their core business of handling emergency situations and legal protection, improve delivery efficiency through better targeting and specialized and portable assistance, and focus on coordination with national governments to ease transitions to inclusive systems.

Donor institutions will have to accept that caring for refugees, particularly in protracted situations, is a development agenda. They will need to adjust their financing instruments and investment models to better support host countries and the self-reliance agenda.

Figure 5.3   Key Elements to Promoting Refugee Self-Reliance

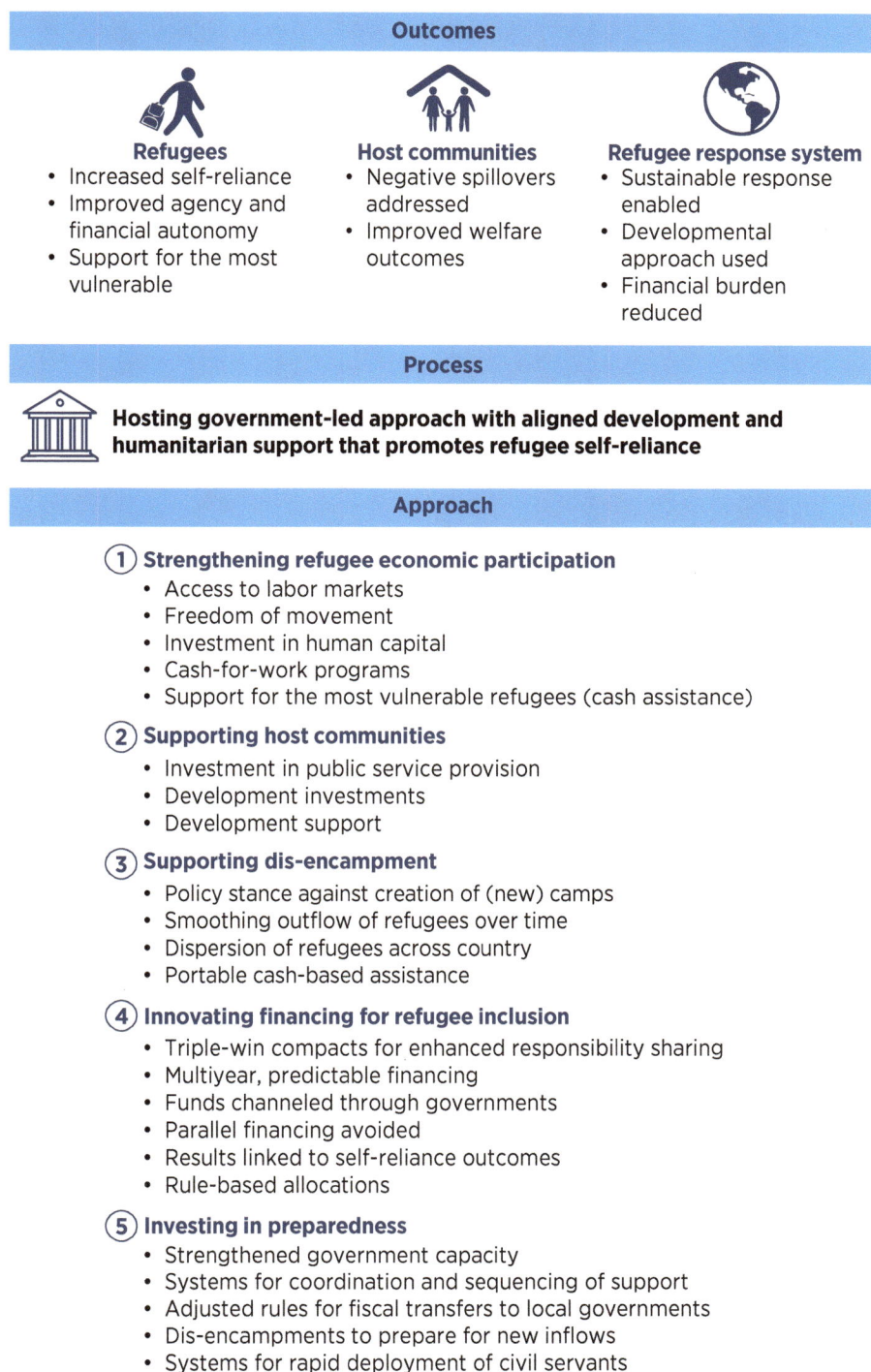

Outcomes

Refugees
- Increased self-reliance
- Improved agency and financial autonomy
- Support for the most vulnerable

Host communities
- Negative spillovers addressed
- Improved welfare outcomes

Refugee response system
- Sustainable response enabled
- Developmental approach used
- Financial burden reduced

Process

Hosting government-led approach with aligned development and humanitarian support that promotes refugee self-reliance

Approach

① **Strengthening refugee economic participation**
- Access to labor markets
- Freedom of movement
- Investment in human capital
- Cash-for-work programs
- Support for the most vulnerable refugees (cash assistance)

② **Supporting host communities**
- Investment in public service provision
- Development investments
- Development support

③ **Supporting dis-encampment**
- Policy stance against creation of (new) camps
- Smoothing outflow of refugees over time
- Dispersion of refugees across country
- Portable cash-based assistance

④ **Innovating financing for refugee inclusion**
- Triple-win compacts for enhanced responsibility sharing
- Multiyear, predictable financing
- Funds channeled through governments
- Parallel financing avoided
- Results linked to self-reliance outcomes
- Rule-based allocations

⑤ **Investing in preparedness**
- Strengthened government capacity
- Systems for coordination and sequencing of support
- Adjusted rules for fiscal transfers to local governments
- Dis-encampments to prepare for new inflows
- Systems for rapid deployment of civil servants

Source: Original figure created for this report.

Annex 5A. Policy Matrix for Greater Refugee Self-Reliance

Table 5A.1   Policy Matrix for Greater Refugee Self-Reliance

	Host governments	Humanitarian agencies	Development agencies
Create an enabling environment Adopt inclusive policies.	• Adopt laws and implementation decrees in support of self-reliance. • Take a policy stance against the creation of (new) camps. • Close existing camps (gradually). • Negotiate a "refugee compact."	• Focus on legal protection and emergency assistance.	• Support development policy financing. • Negotiate a "'refugee compact."
Protect the most vulnerable.		• Provide targeted assistance. • Provide specialized services.	
Strengthen national systems.	• Include parallel service provision in national systems. • Strengthen capacity of key line ministries to incorporate refugees in national systems.	• Close existing camps for those able to work.	• Prioritize investment projects to locations that include refugees. • Strengthen capacity of key line ministries.
Ensure rule-based, predictable aid allocation.	• Advocate for new financing model. • Strengthen monitoring systems.		• Develop new financing model. • Encourage P4R financing for recurrent spending.
Improve emergency preparedness.	• Close existing camps as a means to strengthen capacity. • Adjust fiscal rules. • Create a preparedness plan.	• Create rapid registration systems.	• Develop a rule-based financing model that reflects number of refugees.

(continued)

Table 5A.1 Policy Matrix for Greater Refugee Self-Reliance *(continued)*

	Host governments	Humanitarian agencies	Development agencies
Avoid negative spillovers Disperse refugees.	• Create a refugee relocation program. • Prioritize investment activities in locations ready to include refugees.	• Focus on repatriation and resettlement.	• Prioritize investment activities in locations ready to include refugees.
Smooth refugee flows over time.	• Develop temporary workfare. • Invest in area-based development around camps. • Cap refugee outflows.	• Create time-bound refugee reception centers.	• Develop temporary workfare. • Invest in economic opportunities around camps.

Invest in locations where refugees settle.	• Create investment programs in
	  ◦ Agriculture,
	  ◦ Infrastructure,
	  ◦ Digital infrastructure,
	  ◦ Housing,
	  ◦ Social services and WASH, and
	  ◦ Jobs and public works.
	• Negotiate a "refugee compact."
			• Create investment programs in
			  ◦ Agriculture,
			  ◦ Infrastructure,
			  ◦ Digital infrastructure,
			  ◦ Housing,
			  ◦ Social services and WASH, and
			  ◦ Jobs and public works.
			• Negotiate a "refugee compact."

Strengthen the ability of refugees to settle elsewhere Make assistance portable.	• Provide access to public health and education. • Grant rights to bank accounts. • Invest in digital payment systems. • Strengthen national social protection systems.	• Switch to cash-based assistance for those able to work. • End location-based assistance for those able to work.	• Invest in including refugees in national health and education systems. • Invest in financial inclusion. • Invest in digital payment systems. • Strengthen national social protection systems.

(continued)

Table 5A.1 Policy Matrix for Greater Refugee Self-Reliance *(continued)*

	Host governments	Humanitarian agencies	Development agencies
Support labor market potential of refugees.	• Grant the right to work. • Grant the right to move freely. • Enable access to land.	• Develop training programs. • Provide start-up support.	• Develop training programs. • Provide start-up support. • Restore productive capacity for those able to work.
Include refugees in national systems.	• Adopt laws and implementation decrees in support of refugees' inclusion in national systems. • Include humanitarian schools in national systems. • Include humanitarian health facilities in national systems. • Include refugee registration into national registration systems. • Develop adequate reporting systems.	• Transition students into national systems. • Transition patients into national systems. • Transition refugee registration into national systems.	• Support sector ministries. • Enable financing for recurrent spending.

Source: Original table compiled for this report.

Note: P4R = Program for Results; WASH = water, sanitation, and hygiene.

Notes

1. Similarly, integrating refugees in national schools and health care systems—rather than maintaining parallel services—would improve efficiency and free up resources.
2. Developed economies should be able to cover the cost of hosting out of their own means; the poorest economies have the strongest claim on the available grant financing, and middle-income countries may have only a share of their costs covered through a combination of grants and concessional financing. IDA has such a mechanism, with only the poorest countries eligible for grants, wealthier countries eligible for a combination of concessional loans and grants, and even wealthier countries graduating to the World Bank's International Bank for Reconstruction and Development window of (less) concessional loans.
3. More challenging may be to adjust the financing modality. Donors often seem to have a preference for investments in infrastructure, for example.
4. Betts (2021) reports that 60 percent of Somali refugees residing in Kampala are actually registered as living in one of the country's refugee settlements, because it allows them access to in-kind assistance in the camps, which is not available otherwise. For Dollo Addo, a refugee camp in Ethiopia, Betts and Collier (2019) estimate that the number of refugees actually residing there is approximately one-half of those formerly registered with UNHCR.
5. Congestion tends to be less when refugees are more dispersed and vanishes with time—and at a greater rate when the economy is more dynamic (Rozo and Sviatschi 2021). Nevertheless, a large inflow of refugees to specific locations can have negative repercussions on public services, for the availability of housing, for the price of goods, and for host community job markets.
6. This section draws from Devictor (2023).

References

Anti, Sebastian, Colette Salemi, and Jonathan Rigberg. 2025. "African Refugee Camp and Settlement Dataset: 2025 Update." Unpublished data set prepared for *Making Refugee Self-Reliance Work: From Aid to Employment in Sub-Saharan Africa*, World Bank, Washington, DC.

Baseler, Travis, Thomas Ginn, Robert Hakiza, Helidah Ogude-Chambert, and Olivia Woldemikael. 2025. "Can Redistribution Change Policy Views? Aid and Attitudes Toward Refugees." *Journal of Political Economy* 133 (4). Just Accepted. https://doi.org/10.1086/736209.

Betts, A. 2021. *The Wealth of Refugees: How Displaced People Can Build Economies*. Oxford University Press.

Betts, A. and Paul Collier. 2019. "Refuge: Transforming a Broken Refugee System." *Journal of Refugee Studies* 32 (1): 166–69.

Desiderio, Maria Vincenza. 2016. *Integrating Refugees into Host Country Labor Markets: Challenges and Policy Options*. Washington, DC: Migration Policy Institute.

Devictor, Xavier. 2023. "Many Refugee Shocks Can Be Predicted—and We Can Prepare for Them." *Development for Peace* (blog), October 30, 2023. https://blogs.worldbank .org/en/dev4peace/many-refugee-shocks-can-be-predicted-and-we-can-prepare -them.

OECD (Organisation for Economic Co-operation and Development). 2023. "Development Finance for Refugee Situations: Volumes and Trends, 2020–21." OECD Publishing, Paris. https://www.oecd.org/content/dam/oecd/en/publications/reports/2023/11 /development-finance-for-refugee-situations-volume-and-trends-2020 -2021_46c7725d/cc2df199-en.pdf.

Rozo, Sandra V., and Micaela Sviatschi. 2021. "Is a Refugee Crisis a Housing Crisis? Only if Housing Supply is Unresponsive." *Journal of Development Economics* 148: 102563.

UNHCR (United Nations High Commission for Refugees). 2014. "A Global Strategy for Livelihoods: A UNHCR Strategy 2014–2018." UNHCR, Geneva. https://www.unhcr.org /sites/default/files/legacy-pdf/530f107b6.pdf.

UNHCR. 2018. "Global Compact on Refugees." United Nations, New York. https://www .unhcr.org/us/about-unhcr/who-we-are/global-compact-refugees.

UNHCR (United Nations High Commissioner for Refugees). 2023. "2023 Global Compact on Refugees Indicator Report." UNHCR, Geneva. https://www.unhcr.org/sites/default /files/2023-11/2023-gcr-indicator-report.pdf.

UNHCR (United Nations High Commissioner for Refugees). 2025. "Sustainable Programming: What Is Sustainable Programming and Why Is It Needed?" UNHCR, Geneva. https://data.unhcr.org/en/documents/details/114423.

UNHCR (United Nations High Commission for Refugees) and World Bank. 2024. "The Global Cost of Refugee Inclusion in Host Countries' Health Systems." World Bank, Washington, DC.

World Bank. 2023. "The Global Cost of Inclusive Refugee Education: 2023 Update." World Bank, Washington, DC.

World Bank. n.d. "The Refugee Policy Review Framework." Technical Note, World Bank, Washington, DC.

Zetter, Roger, and Héloïse Ruaudel. 2016. "Refugees' Right to Work and Access to Labor Markets—An Assessment." KNOMAD Working Paper and Study Series, Global Knowledge Partnership on Migration and Development, World Bank, Washington, DC.

APPENDIX A
Background Papers and Data Sets Prepared for this Report

Abeje, Fikirte, Cesar Cancho, and Johannes Hoogeveen. 2025. "The Case for Ethiopia's Refugee Jobs Compact Remains." Background paper for *Making Refugee Self-Reliance Work: From Aid to Employment in Sub-Saharan Africa*. World Bank, Washington, DC.

Anti, Sebastian, Colette Salemi, and Jonathan Rigberg. 2025. "African Refugee Camp and Settlement Dataset: 2025 Update." World Bank, Washington, DC.

Atamanov, Aziz, Johannes Hoogeveen, and Benjamin Reese. 2024. "The Costs Come Before the Benefits: Why Donors Should Invest More in Refugee Autonomy in Uganda." Policy Research Working Paper 10679, World Bank, Washington, DC.

Coulibaly, Mohamed, Johannes Hoogeveen, Emilie Jourdan, and Aboudrahyme Savadogo. 2024. "Responsibility Sharing and the Economic Participation of Refugees in Chad." Policy Research Working Paper 10727, World Bank, Washington, DC.

Coulibaly, Mohammed, Johannes Hoogeveen, Robert Hopper, and Aboudrahyme Savadogo. 2025. "Towards More Sustainable Solutions for the Forcibly Displaced in Niger." Background paper for *Making Refugee Self-Reliance Work: From Aid to Employment in Sub-Saharan Africa*. World Bank, Washington, DC.

Hoogeveen, Johannes, and Robert Hopper. 2024. "Using Poverty Lines to Measure Refugee Self-Reliance." Policy Research Working Paper 10910, World Bank, Washington, DC.

Hoogeveen, Johannes, Sebastian Leander, and Olive Nsababera. 2024. "Unpacking Spatial Variations in Refugee Self-Reliance in Kenya." Background paper for *Making Refugee Self-Reliance Work: From Aid to Employment in Sub-Saharan Africa*. World Bank, Washington, DC.

Hoogeveen, Johannes, Robert Hopper, and Jonathan Lain. 2025. "Measuring Multi-Dimensional Self-Reliance for Refugees and IDPs, with an Application to Niger and CAR." Background paper for *Making Refugee Self-Reliance Work: From Aid to Employment in Sub-Saharan Africa*. World Bank, Washington, DC.

Sarzin, Zara, and Olive Nsababera 2024. "Forced Displacement in Sub-Saharan Africa: A Stocktaking of Evidence." Background Paper for the Africa Region Companion Report to *World Bank 2023: Migrants, Refugees, and Societies*. World Bank, Washington, DC.

www.ingramcontent.com/pod-product-compliance
Lightning Source LLC
Chambersburg PA
CBHW041239020426
42333CB00002B/19

* 9 7 8 1 4 6 4 8 1 9 6 9 8 *